EXTREME
BUGS

D1469945

EXTREME BUGS. Copyright © 2007 by HarperCollins Publishers. All rights reserved. Printed in the United States of America. No part of this book may be used or reproduced in any manner whatsoever without written permission except in the case of brief quotations embodied in critical articles and reviews. For information, address HarperCollins Publishers, 10 East 53rd Street, New York, NY 10022.

HarperCollins books may be purchased for educational, business, or sales promotional use. For information, please write: Special Markets Department, HarperCollins Publishers, 10 East 53rd Street, New York, NY 10022.

Produced for HarperCollins by:

HYDRA PUBLISHING
129 MAIN STREET
IRVINGTON, NY 10533
WWW.HYLASPUBLISHING.COM

FIRST EDITION

The name of the "Smithsonian," "Smithsonian Institution," and the sunburst logo are registered trademarks of the Smithsonian Institution.

Library of Congress Cataloging-in-Publication Data

Mertz, Leslie A.
  Extreme bugs / Leslie Mertz. — 1st ed.
      p. cm.
  Includes index.
  ISBN 978-0-06-089147-3
  1. Insects. I. Title.

QL463.M48 2007
595.7—dc22

                              2007023017

07 08 09 10   QW   10 9 8 7 6 5 4 3 2 1

EXTREME
BUGS

Collins

An Imprint of HarperCollinsPublishers

Leslie Mertz

Boca Raton Public Library, Boca Raton, FL

Contents

What Is an Insect?

Ants and beetles, dragonflies and moths, termites and mosquitoes—they hardly look alike, yet they are all insects. Spiders, ticks, and roly-polies, however, are not insects. So what makes an insect an insect?

Three Segments

First, all insects have three distinct body parts: a head; a chest, known as a thorax; and an abdomen. In most insects, the three parts are readily identifiable because they noticeably narrow where adjacent parts meet. Both the thorax and abdomen are made up of usually obvious segments. In fact, the word *insect* comes from the Latin word for "notched" or "segmented."

The Thorax

The thorax has three segments in a row from front to back. Each segment bears a pair of legs, for a total of 6. Spiders and ticks have 8 legs, and roly-polies have 14, so none of these creatures qualify as insects. Most insects also have two pairs of wings, one pair sprouting from each of the last two thoracic segments. Although it may appear that the legs and wings come from the abdomen of some insects, especially when the wings completely blanket the abdomen, a closer look will verify that they originate at the thorax.

The Abdomen

An insect's abdomen has up to 11 segments, although they may be hidden from view by the wings. In beetles, the hard forewings can lie so closely on the abdomen that they appear to be a part of it. The abdomen contains most of the insect's inner workings, including the heart and reproductive organs.

The Head

The head, on the other hand, houses the majority of the sensory equipment, including a pair of antennae that feels, tastes, and smells. Insects may have five eyes—two large conspicuous and sometimes enormous compound eyes, and up to three pinprick-sized simple eyes between them. The head also contains the brain, but the insect's brain is little like that of a human. Whereas the human brain is a complex collection of nervous tissue that nearly fills the skull, the insect brain is a combination of three nerve clusters called ganglia that take up little of the space

Members of the Hymenoptera order, such as this wasp, display the three distinct segments that identify them as insects.

Opposite: A close-up view of a mantid shows the large compound eyes typical of insects.

in the head. One of the ganglia mainly handles vision, another primarily takes care of sensory input from the antennae, and the third oversees most of the other internal organs. Besides these nerve clusters, other ganglia elsewhere in the body control the muscles, as well as the movements of the legs and wings. The small, simple ganglia (compared to so-called higher animals) give an insect a machinelike quality. Its brain processes various stimuli and triggers a reaction. For example, light may be the stimulus for an underground-living insect to run for cover. Like a machine that always does the same thing when prompted, an insect does not mull over its options; it just reacts.

As well as the physical characteristics of three body parts, six legs, and two antennae that adult insects share, they also have another incontrovertibly nonhuman trait. Instead of a spinal column and other bones resting inside the body and muscle tissue lying on top, insects wear an external skeletal coat, an exoskeleton, that encloses all of their muscle and other soft tissue. The hard exoskeleton, made of a fingernail-like substance, is broken into plates and has flexible material between to permit quite a full range of motion, yet afford a good deal of protection.

Infinite Diversity

Despite their basic similarities, insects are amazingly diverse creatures. The smallest are minuscule parasitic wasps (*Dicopomorpha echmepterygis* and *Megaphragma caribea*) measuring 0.005 to 0.007 inches (0.014–0.017 cm) in body length, while the longest, a walkingstick known by the scientific name of *Pharnacia serratipes*, can reach a startling 22 inches (55.9 cm) from the tips of its forward-stretched front legs to the ends of its rearward-extended hind legs. Wingspan is another wide-ranging variable among insect species. Some species have enormous wings. They include the white witch (*Thysania agrippina*), a black-etched white moth with an impressive wingspan of up to 11 inches (28 cm). Insects grew even larger in prehistoric times. The largest insect ever known to inhabit Earth was a dragonfly-like insect (*Meganeura*

One of the "long-horned" members of the Coleoptera order, the *Anoplophora zonatrix* beetle uses its enormous antennae to feel around its environment.

monyi) with a body length of 18 inches (46 cm) and a wingspan of two and a half feet (76 cm). It existed about 250 million years ago. At the other end of the size spectrum fall currently living insects such as the minuscule parasitic wasps called fairyflies (in the genus *Alaptus*), some of which have wingspans of just 0.008 inches (0.02 cm).

This diversity extends far beyond size to myriad outward characteristics, lifestyles, reproductive strategies, developmental pathways, and other features. A few are:

- antennae length and style, including feathery, filamentous, combed, and many others;
- mouthpart type, ranging from chewing to sucking and lapping to piercing;
- number of wings, which may be four, two, or none;
- style of wings, varying from membranous to leathery or hardened, and broad to narrow;
- primary mode of transportation, including flying, running, walking, swimming, and water-surface skating;
- and the production of young from male-fertilized eggs, or from unfertilized eggs.

The great variety becomes mind-boggling when considering the vast number of insects that live on Earth today. Other currently known inhabitants of the planet include approximately 250,000 species of flowering plants and trees; 25,000 species of fishes; 10,000 species of birds; and 5,000 species of mammals, among others. Insects outnumber them all. Scientists now count about 900,000 known insect species, and entomologists believe hundreds of thousands—and probably millions—still await discovery.

Insects are different from humans, and indeed from every other type of organism on Earth. The following pages will explore their beauty and their strangeness, as well as the characteristics that set them apart and make them so intriguing.

Above: Commonly known as the white witch moth, *Thysania agrippina* has an impressive wingspan—nearly a foot long in some individuals.

Below: Insects come in incredible colors and forms. This walkingstick of Southeast Asia sports colorful wings that can be folded down when the insect wants to blend in with the surrounding foliage.

PART 1

INSECT IDENTITY

CHAPTER 1

NATURAL BEAUTIES

INSECTS MAY NOT BE THE FIRST THINGS that come to mind when describing an idyllic natural scene, but does anything quite put an exclamation point on a summer day like a marvelously colored butterfly fluttering down to alight gently on a wildflower or cap an evening like a ghostly and graceful moth perching motionless on a window screen? Almost any sweep through a meadow with an insect net will yield insects of nearly every color of the spectrum, in sizes ranging from microscopic to bean-sized and often even larger. Peer through a magnifying glass at the multifaceted eye of a dragonfly or the detail of an antenna and the exquisiteness of the insect world comes sharply into focus. The variety in wing patterns alone could take days to describe. The following pages provide a small sampling of the diverse insects that make their homes in diverse places around the globe. Beauty may be in the eye of the beholder, but all of the insects listed here have spectacular colors, patterns, shapes, or other features that make them extreme pleasures to behold.

Left: A butterfly need not be brilliantly colored to be striking, as this paperkite *(Idea leuconoe)*, with its elegant wings of black and white, demonstrates. Inset: Butterflies may be symbols of beauty, but their moth cousins are no less awe-inspiring. Pages 4–5: An iridescent Japanese beetle. From the flamboyant to the plain, beetles come in seemingly infiinite variations.

Butterfly Diversity

Large or small, plain or patterned, butterflies are usually at the top of the list of most beautiful insects. One that is often hailed as the world's most stunning is the blue morpho (*Morpho didius*). With a wingspan of about 7 inches (18 cm) and iridescent blue wings edged with deep brown, it dazzles in the rain forests of its native Central and South America. The color is so spectacular that pilots flying close to the trees can even spot cerulean flashes as the flapping wings catch the sunlight. The undersides of the wings are mainly a muted brown patterned with white, so at rest, when the wings are folded closed and only the undersides show, the morpho blends into the surrounding trees. Even when airborne, as it opens and shuts its wings, it reveals only quick glimpses of blue. Combined with its weaving flight, the here-and-gone blue wings make the butterfly quite difficult for a person, or for a would-be predator, to track through the forest.

The intricate patterns displayed when the blue morpho butterfly holds its wings closed belie the striking blue color of its other side (see page 17). This is one of the several species in Central and South America.

A Rainbow of Hues

Another colorful and striking butterfly is South America's Apollo metalmark (*Lyropteryx apollonia*). Like those of many other metalmark species in its family, portions of its wings are reflective. In this species, the wings display alternating, thin black and shimmering turquoise stripes radiating from the body to the tips of its wings. The base of each lower wing sports a bright pink dot. The undersides of the wings mimic the topsides, but the bases are crowded with pink spots.

Many other butterflies have wings with a surprisingly different appearance from one side to the other. One is the South American species known by its scientific name of *Callicore hesperis*. From above, the wings are black with wide gleaming sapphire and cherry streaks. On the underside, the front wing is black with a cherry streak, but also flaunts a cream-colored bar and a thin ribbon of sky blue. The underside of the hind wing is black streaked with cream and a bit of blue, and dotted with pops of white outlined in baby blue.

Gorgeous butterflies extend beyond the Southern Hemisphere. An example of a North American head-turner is the California sister (*Adelpha bredowii*), a butterfly of the western United States. With a 2.5 to 3.5 inch (6.4–8.9 cm) wingspan, it draws notice. The upper surfaces of its dark-chocolate wings showcase a thick, incomplete, cream-colored stripe in the center, and a few more dapples of cream lying along a

"Butterflies . . . not quite birds, as they were not quite flowers, mysterious and fascinating as are all indeterminate creatures."

—ELIZABETH GOUDGE

bright orange splash on the tip of the forewing. The underside has the same flaming orange patch, but the similarity ends there. Lilac blue, orange, and light tan markings mingle with brown to create a swirling pattern.

The Swallowtails

A listing of lovely butterflies would hardly be complete without mention of the swallowtails. Nearly every one of the more than 600 species worldwide could qualify as one of the planet's most attractive. Nearly all of the members of this family have ample wings, as well as projections extending from the ends of their hind wings. Those with the longest projections call to mind the sweeping tail feathers of swallows and give this group of butterflies its common name. Some of the most stunning U.S. species include the giant swallowtail (*Papilio cresphontes*) with its ebony and bold-yellow wings, the zebra swallowtail (*Eurytides marcellus*) with roughly the same pattern as its namesake, and the pipevine swallowtail (*Battus philenor*) with midnight-black forewings and iridescent blue hind wings. The giant

NATURE'S LEDs

In 2005, scientists found that the scales of a certain swallowtail, *Princeps nireus*, were surprisingly similar to a new-generation, ultra-high-performance light-emitting diode (LED)—the devices that provide the illumination for such things as computer and television screens. Physicist Pete Vukusic of Exeter University in England reported that extreme close-ups of individual scales on the male's unusual fluorescent wings revealed the same complex structure that makes the new LEDs several times brighter than the old. Magnified images of the scales show not only fluorescent pigment, but also an extensive system of scaffolding that intensifies light reflection. Together the nature-engineered scaffolding and the pigment produce the butterfly's brilliant blue-green sheen when viewed under UV light. The males' wings are believed to be an advertisement to females at mating time.

swallowtail and its wingspan that can stretch up to 5.5 inches (14 cm) wide make it the largest of the three. The other two species have wingspans of about 3.4 to 3.5 inches (8.6–8.9 cm).

Above left: One of the most beautiful butterflies in North America, the giant swallowtail is also the largest American butterfly. Its range extends as far as Canada and South America.

Left: The metallic blue-and-black pipevine swallowtail ranges from the southern United States to Mexico.

Moth Diversity

Although moths can have exquisitely hued wings and sometimes enormous size, they do not garner the same admiration as butterflies. Part of the reason is their preference for the night. Unless a large one lands on a lighted window, people roundly ignore these mainly after-hours insects. Two North American species, however, have attained star status: the cecropia moth and the polyphemus moth.

Nighttime Enchanters

With a wingspan of about half a foot (15 cm), the cecropia moth (*Hyalophora cecropia*) is the largest on the continent. Its olive-colored wings each display an ivory-and-orange crescent moon, and the outer margin is detailed in peach, white, and olive markings. A large dark eyespot—so called because it is thought to resemble a large eye—adorns the front of each leading wing. Like many moths, and unlike butterflies, the cecropia has a plump, furry-looking body and feathery antennae and rests with its wings outspread. Its body size is accentuated by a blanket of white and orange-red hair. Butterflies have nonfuzzy and svelter bodies and thin antennae, each one usually tipped with a small knob. In addition, most butterflies rest with their wings folded in an upright position, which leaves only the undersides of their wings visible.

Above: The distinctive crescent-moon shape is evident on both sides of the cecropia moth's four wings.

Right: Identifying features of the luna moth are its luminous pale-green color and the extended "tails" on its hind wings.

The polyphemus moth (*Anthera polyphemus*) has a wingspan about a half inch smaller than the cecropia, but has an eyespot on each of its four wings. The tiny eyespots on the front wings are dwarfed by the enormous black, blue, and yellow pair on the hind wings. Depending on the individual, its wings may be olive or tan with a paler-colored margin. On the undersides, the wings are shades of brown in a pattern much like tree bark. A similar moth from Europe, parts of Asia, and the Middle East is the great peacock moth (*Saturnia pyri*), which has a wingspan comparable to that of the cecropia and an appearance similar to the polyphemus, except that all of its four eyespots are large.

The Luna Moth

Another good-sized species from North America that draws attention is the luna moth (*Actias luna*), with delicate, swallowtailed wings that resemble shaved slices of light-green stained glass. The leading edge of each front wing bears brown piping, and each of

"Hurt no living thing: Ladybird, nor butterfly, Nor moth with dusty wing."

—CHRISTINA GEORGINA ROSSETTI

its four wings has a small circular or kiss-shaped eyespot. This species can attain a wingspan of about 5 inches (12.7 cm). As with the cecropia, polyphemus, and many other moths, the adult luna moth lives a very short time. This is because adults of many species either have nonfunctional mouths or lack mouths completely. Even without the ability to eat, however, they are able to survive long enough—a few days to a couple of weeks—to mate and begin the next generation of moths.

The Madagascar Moon Moth and Other Beauties

Yet another standout, this time from the Southern Hemisphere, is the Madagascar moon moth (*Argema mittrei*), which has a butter-yellow hue and sweeping wing tails. The wingspan is 5.5 inches (14 cm), but with wings outstretched from front to back it measures a whopping 8 to 10 inches (20.3–25.4 cm) long from the leading edge of the forewings to the tip of the hind wings' tails. As the luna moth does, the moon moth often rests with its "tails" overlapping or crossed, giving it a graceful appearance.

Some other lovely species include the tiger moths. Various species of these live nearly everywhere in the world. They typically have intricate

forewing patterns, often a mosaic of black and cream with orange or crimson hind wings. One of the largest, the great leopard moth (*Hypercompe scribonia*), has brilliant white forewings covered with black rings and spots of varying sizes, white hind wings, a black-spotted white thorax, and a metallic-blue abdomen. This species resides in the eastern half of the United States.

Above: The Madagascar moon moth is also known as a comet moth.

Below: For thousands of years, people around the world have made collections of colorful and unusual moths and butterflies.

INSECT COLLECTORS

Insect collecting has grown into much more than a hobby performed by enthusiasts running through fields and forests with nets. Especially when beautiful and unusual butterflies and moths are concerned, it has spawned commercial businesses, including butterfly farms that buy and sell live insects as well as mounted butterflies and moth specimens to zoos and other facilities, and to private collectors the world over. On the seedier side, the commercial value of butterflies and moths has also drawn poachers. Although such activities are rare, poaching operations in U.S. national parks have led to arrests and convictions. In one of the largest cases, three men pleaded guilty in the mid-1990s to taking more than 2,200 butterflies, including 210 endangered species, from five national parks. Some of the rarer butterflies could have fetched several hundred dollars.

Lacewings

In this close-up of a lacewing, the insect's characteristically large, round eyes are hard to miss.

Butterflies and moths do not corner the market on good looks. Two other groups of insects—one graceful and the other more lumbering—draw raves. *Graceful* describes the lacewings, insects with long, mainly transparent wings that recall the fine and delicate lace of a bridal veil. On the other hand, *lumbering* better portrays many of the beetles, a vast group of creatures that come in a great variety of shapes and colors.

Delicate Fliers

Many people, and gardeners in particular, are familiar with green lacewings, which flit in Tinkerbell-like fashion from plant to plant. Although a number of species exist around the world, all of them have a similar appearance. Huge and nearly invisible wings stretch well past the ends of their thin and long, pale-lime-green bodies. The head has two large, dark, sometimes golden eyes and fine antennae that are about as long as the body. Several species live

in North America, and an especially wide-ranging one (*Chrysoperla plorabunda*) extends from coast to coast and from Canada to Mexico. As with many other lacewings, this one has an extremely soft, thumping call reminiscent of a heartbeat. Another green lacewing, this species from Europe and parts of Asia, has a faster call that duplicates the sound of a far-off outboard motor. In both cases, the insects produce the calls by vibrating the abdomen. Without a keen ear almost touching the lacewing, however, people are typically unaware that the insects make any noise at all.

A few lacewings are downright jaw-dropping. Some of the most dramatic are known as ribbon or thread-winged lacewings. These species have the typical large forewings, although some carry patterns of brown and yellow or ivory, but their hind wings seem as if they have been pulled like taffy into long, narrow versions of their former selves. An example is the thread-winged lacewing (*Nemoptera sinuata*) from Turkey. Its hind wings, which are extremely thin at the base and widen only slightly toward the rear, are three times the length of its body. With front wings stretched to either side and hind wings extended backward, the insect is about 1.8 inches (4.6 cm) wide and 2.4 inches (6.1 cm) long. The somewhat

similar-looking spoon-winged lacewings (in the genus *Chasmoptera*) from southwestern Australia have slightly shorter hind wings that flaunt a bit wider flare at the tips.

Above: Resembling many-paned windows, the net-veined wings on this green lacewing provide a frame for the insect's body below.

Left: Large, ornate forewings and long, pencil-thin hind wings are hallmarks of the thread-winged lacewing, which makes its home in Turkey.

Beetle Diversity

For the beetles, human attention usually comes in the form of the bottom of a shoe, but for the person who takes the time for a closer inspection, many are quite fabulous.

If color makes an insect attractive, the rainbow leaf beetle (*Chrysolina cerealis*) of Europe is dazzling. Growing to only 0.3 to 0.4 inches (8–10 mm) long, this oval-shaped beetle makes up for its small size with shiny stripes of red, blue, green, and yellow running from head to tail end. It is a rare beetle and even considered endangered in Great Britain, where it is found on the flowers of wild thyme plants in high-altitude grasslands. Another small, but jewel-like beetle is a flower beetle, *Gymnetis pantherina*, of South America. This insect, which grows to about twice the size of the rainbow leaf beetle, is orangish yellow speckled with a mirror-image maze of black specks on its right and left sides and forward onto the top of its head. Another dazzling specimen, this time in rich green and gold and measuring about an inch (2.5 cm) in length, is the aptly named glorious beetle (*Chrysina gloriosa*) of northern Mexico and the American Southwest. Even its underside is eye-catching in shimmering copper with horizontal green stripes on the abdomen.

In all three of these species, as well as the vast majority of other beetles, their showy backs are mainly composed of their hard front wings, called elytra, that cover all or most of the abdomen. A second pair of filmy and usually larger hind wings remain folded up and hidden beneath the elytra, only making their presence known when the beetle takes flight. At that point, the elytra lift out of the way and the hind wings spread to their full size to take the beetle skyward.

Splashes of Color

Blue is a fairly rare color among beetles, but a few weevils from Papua New Guinea are azure knockouts. Three of the most colorful are closely related weevils known simply as blue weevils (*Eupholus magnificus, Eupholus bennetti,* and *Eupholus quintaenia*). Each of these approximately inch-long (2.5 cm), vivid blue beetles is emblazoned with a black or black-and-white motif and has the characteristically long snout associated with nearly all weevils.

Above: The rainbow leaf beetle, considered endangered in Great Britain, where it occurs in only one small area, makes its home throughout much of the rest of Europe.

Right: This vivid-blue weevil of the genus *Eupholus* displays the unusual antennae placement of all weevils, at least halfway down the snout rather than nearer the eyes as is typical in other insects.

"Whenever I hear of the capture of rare beetles, I feel like an old war-horse at the sound of a trumpet."

—CHARLES DARWIN

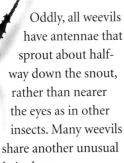

Oddly, all weevils have antennae that sprout about half-way down the snout, rather than nearer the eyes as in other insects. Many weevils share another unusual trait: their elytra are united and their hind wings are missing altogether, making flight impossible.

The family known as metallic wood-boring beetles also go by the more flattering name of jewel beetles. Many of these species are both shiny and colorful. A few, such as the nearly inch-long (2 cm) beetle known by its scientific name of *Julodis viridipes*, have an extra adornment: hairs. This particular beetle, which makes its home in South Africa, has a reflective black back; long, green legs; and periodic tufts of short, yellow hair sprouting from its elytra, thorax, head, and even its underside.

Some of the larger beetles are also beauties. Africa has several examples. One, known by its scientific name of *Chelorrhina polyphemus*, reaches 2.2 inches (5.5 cm). This forest-green beetle's thorax is trimmed with pale-yellow stripes, and its elytra also have a few splashes of the color. Its head has two big eyes peering from either side.

In the male, the head is also equipped with prominent, black-tipped horns. Horns are quite common in males of this group of beetles, known as the scarab family. Typically, males use their horns to fight over females, and the beetle with the largest set wins the girl. Other large, but attractive scarabs are the goliath beetles, also of Africa. One species' elytra are black and cream, but in a pattern that has the effect of crackly paint on a weathered piece of wood. Another has a half-and-half design: maroon on the rear half and bold black and white stripes toward the front. They earn the name "goliath" from their massive size. They can grow to about 4.5 inches (11.4 cm) long— nearly enough to cover a person's hand.

Above left: Unlike female *Chelorrhina polyphemus*, males have horns on the sides and at the front of the head. The size of the horns differs among individual males.

Below: Most dung beetles have no horns, but they do have an unusual behavior: they roll balls of dung.

BEETLEMANIA

If you have ever wondered why ancient Egyptians mummified their dead, look no further than the dung beetle, a member of the Scarabaeidae family. With its habit of rolling balls of feces with its hind feet, it hardly seems idol material; nonetheless, the Egyptians revered it. Their high regard came from observations of its life cycle: the dung beetle buries its ball of dung, a larva soon emerges to live a short time before becoming encased—and dying, in the ancient Egyptians' view—in its leathery pupa, and finally bursting out of its pupa "reborn" as a beetle. They equated this process with the setting, or dying, of the sun at the end of one day and its dawning as a "new" sun the next. The Egyptians applied the process to their dead. They mummified the corpse, a duplication of the beetle's pupal stage, in the hopes that the person would one day be resurrected.

The Orders Up Close

Insects: Butterflies and moths

Order: Lepidoptera

Meaning of Lepidoptera: "scale wing," referring to the tiny, overlapping scales that cover the wings

Typical characteristics of adults in this order:

• a pair each of large, scale-coated forewings and hind wings, although a few moths have no wings

• two large compound eyes

• a pair of long antennae—usually with a clubbed tip in butterflies, and feathery or threadlike in moths

• a mouth fashioned into a coiled tube for sucking nectar from flowers, although in some species the tube is reduced or missing altogether

• a long and rather thin body, especially in butterflies

• the larvae are called caterpillars

DIVERSITY

Number of known species: 150,000–165,000

Size: Wingspan varies from about 0.2 to 11 inches (0.5–28 cm). The smallest are various leaf-miner moths (in the family Nepticulidae). The largest, *Thysania agrippina*, goes by such colorful names as the white witch moth, ghost moth, and great owlet moth, and makes its home from Mexico to South America.

Sampling of benefits to humans: pollination, aesthetic value, commercial worth as collected specimens

Butterflies, such as this variegated fritillary, *Euptoieta claudia*, have a slight to very noticeable thickening, or club, at the end of each antenna. Moths lack the clubs.

The Spanish moon moth, *Graellsia isabellae*, displays the plump, hairy body and feathered antennae common to many moths. Some moths have thin, hair-like antennae instead.

A young Native American girl celebrates the butterfly by performing the traditional Butterfly Dance at the 2005 Cheyenne Frontier Days rodeo, in Wyoming.

THE BUTTERFLY DANCE

Native cultures have historically revered the creatures of Earth, and insects are no exception. Among Native Americans, the Hopi Butterfly Dance stands out. The Hopi, who have lived in what is now the southwestern United States for centuries, still perform the traditional dance today. Adults sing to the beat of drums, and children and teens dance in elaborate and colorful costumes, sometimes donning large headdresses. The tribe performs the dance, which honors the butterfly's role as a pollinator, at the end of the summer to bring rain to the sun-scorched desert of the Southwest.

This giant long-horned beetle can grow to be as long as or longer than an adult human's hand, making it the largest living beetle on the planet.

As the blue morpho flaps its wings, it alternately reveals and conceals the metallic blue of the top surface of its wings. Occupants of low-flying planes can often see flashes of the brilliant color as the insect flies through its tropical rain-forest habitat.

SPECIFICATIONS

Insects: Beetles

Order: Coleoptera

Meaning of Coleoptera: "sheath wing," referring to the hard front wings that typically cover all or most of the beetle's abdomen

Typical characteristics of adults in this order:

- hard forewings that cover the filmy, usually larger hind wings that remain folded and concealed until taking flight
- rather short antennae, although some have antennae longer than the body
- noticeable and sometimes huge jaws
- the larvae are typically known as grubs

DIVERSITY

Number of known species: 300,000–350,000

Size: Body length ranges from about 0.01 inches (0.25 mm) in the tiny fringed ant beetle (*Nanosella fungi*) to 6 to 7 inches (15–18 cm) in the giant long-horned beetle (*Titanus giganteus*) of South America.

Sampling of benefits to humans: often are predators of insects, including some pest species, and some are decomposers; prey for other animals, including human in some cultures

SPECIFICATIONS

Insects: Lacewings and antlions

Order: Neuroptera

Meaning of Neuroptera: "nerve wing" or "vein wing," referring to the netlike branching in their wings

Typical characteristics of adults in this order:

- two pairs of similarly sized, large, broad wings that rest in tentlike fashion above the abdomen and extend well beyond it
- lacelike pattern in the wings due to interconnecting veins
- the leading edge of each wing broken by numerous veins into a row of small, square cells
- a pair of conspicuous, round compound eyes
- two long, thin antennae
- the larvae of many species are called antlions or doodlebugs

DIVERSITY

Number of known species: about 5,500–6,000

Size: Depending on the species, body length ranges from about 0.4 inches (1 cm) in several species to 6.3 inches (16 cm) in the especially large members of the genus *Palpares* of Madagascar and the African continent.

Sampling of benefits to humans: predators of agricultural pest insects

TRICK OF THE LIGHT

Butterfly and moth scales are the bits of "dust" that rub off when touching a wing. The wing's color comes from the scales. Sometimes the scales are actually colored, but sometimes they are not—even though they can appear brightly hued. The morpho is an example of a butterfly with scales that are not themselves blue, but still produce a brilliant blue sheen. This is accomplished through tiny structures within each scale that reflect certain wavelengths of incoming light. When light strikes the morpho's scales, the wings appear blue.

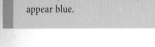

Antlions have long wings, somewhat like those of dragonflies, but they are much slower and far less maneuverable fliers.

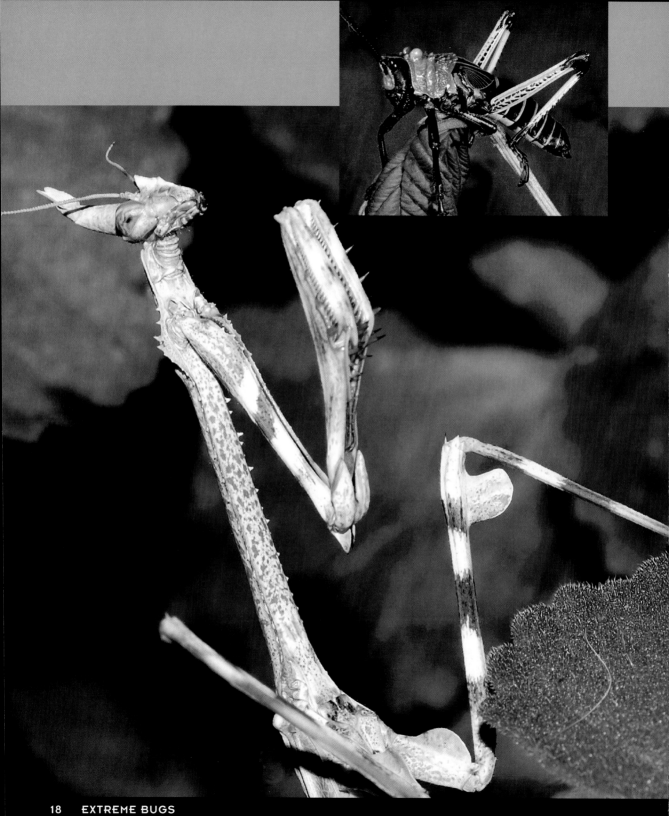

CHAPTER 2

JUST BIZARRE

FOR ALL OF THE BEAUTIFUL SPECIES in the insect world, "bizarre" is the better adjective of choice for quite a few of them. All insects have their "weird" features when viewed up close, but some species repeatedly draw comments such as: "What in the world is that?" and of course, "Kill it!" Unfortunately, many people never take a close look at an insect until after they have squashed it. Although all groups of insects have their share of off-the-wall members, a few seem to corner the market on the peculiar. Among the three groups noted below are species such as mole crickets with shovel-shaped front legs, demon crickets with their tusked jaws, toe-biters that do just that to unlucky waders, mantids with a threat display not soon forgotten, beetles shaped like banjos, and a predacious, subterranean grub that reaches up to snatch land-living insects and drag them underground to devour them there. These examples, however, are just a small sampling. Similarly bizarre six-legged creatures lurk in parks and backyards, woods and fields, as well as homes and other buildings the world over.

Left: The swiveling, large-eyed head and rasping forelegs of the praying mantid may be the features that make it a model for science-fiction aliens. Inset: Why do many people find insects "creepy"? Is it the six legs and their mechanical movements, the pupil-less eyes, or the completely nonhuman antennae?

Order Orthoptera

In the past, curious folks carrying jars or bags containing sometimes living and sometimes dead insects visited the offices of entomologists seeking help in identifying their prizes. Today, people snap digital photographs and visit entomological Web sites instead.

The Mole Cricket

Whatever the method of delivery, one of the most common insects to appear in front of an insect specialist is a creature that usually spends much of its time underground—although it has wings and is capable of flying, sometimes long distances. It looks something like a typical field cricket, but wears an enormous helmet and has shovel-like extensions on its front legs. It is one of the several species of mole cricket (including *Neocurtilla hexadactyla, Gryllotalpa gryllotalpa,* and several others) found quite commonly in North America and Europe. The "helmet" is actually the shield-shaped thorax, which extends forward over the head and backward over at least the first pair of legs. Its hind limbs, although long like a cricket's, are thin and not used for jumping. Instead, the mole cricket uses its powerful, enlarged front legs and its long, massive claws to tunnel just below the surface, much the way that moles do. Its excavations are evident in the same, although smaller, mounds and trails of hilled dirt that moles also make. People

typically encounter mole crickets that are rushing through a damp spot of ground, sometimes floating dead in a swimming pool, or racing for cover when their hiding spot under a rock has been exposed. Mostly, though, mole crickets make their presence known through a series of short, two-chirped phrases at night, or by way of the dirt mounds or inadvertently unearthed seedlings they leave in their wake.

The Jerusalem Cricket

Another strange insect that keeps people guessing in the southwestern United States and Mexico is the Jerusalem cricket (*Stenopalmatus fuscus*). This shiny animal has two beady eyes on an orange bubble of a head and appears as if it is dressed for a formal party. Its unwinged thorax gives the impression of a tall collar, and its ample abdomen is black to dark brown with horizontal white pinstripes. It strikes a somewhat crablike stance with its six slightly pudgy legs held away from the body. Growing to about 2 inches (5.1 cm) long, the Jerusalem cricket shares the mole cricket's penchant for burrowing and usually remains underground during the day. Its other common names are potato bug; stone cricket; *niño de la tierra*, which means "child of the earth" in Spanish; and *woh-tzi-neh*, a Native American word for "old bald-headed man" that refers to

More common than most people realize, the mole cricket is an excavator that lives underground. Some species grow to 2 inches (5.1 cm) long.

Background: In the Maori tongue, this demon grasshopper, or weta, has a name that means "god of ugly things." Although threatening-looking, it very rarely bites people.

its vaguely human-shaped head. Similar species, also called Jerusalem crickets, live in other areas of North America, Central America, Asia, and Africa.

The Weta

Sometimes called "demon grasshoppers," the group of insects known as weta are large, wingless creatures, often with spikes on their large hind legs and massive jaws that are occasionally equipped with tusks. The word *weta* is short for *wetapunga*, a Maori term meaning "god of ugly things." The largest are known as giant weta (several species of the genus *Deinacrida*) and live in New Zealand. They can grow to more than 3 inches (8.5–9 cm) long with their outstretched legs spanning a full 7 inches (18 cm). Like the Jerusalem cricket and mole cricket, they are nocturnal and stay out of sight during the day. For all the ferocity of their jaws, most weta species are herbivorous and rarely bite people. Instead, they flail their spiny hind legs as a defense and

usually only nip if they are physically harassed. Their overall size and appearance alone, however, are enough to keep most humans at bay.

The Katydids

All katydids can be a bit startling, especially when a person is gazing at a leaf that suddenly turns to peer back. The rhinoceros katydid (*Copiphora rhinoceros*), also known as the conehead katydid, however, is a South American insect that always demands a second view. Like most other katydids, when it is not flying, it folds its large wings so that they form a rooflike peak over its back. Measured at rest from the tip of the head to the end of the wings, it is typically about 2.5 inches (6.4 cm) long. The rhinoceros katydid differs from most other katydids and, for that matter, from most other insects by having a pointed horn growing out of the top of its head in a style reminiscent of a rhino.

MIND-CONTROLLING WORMS

Why do some grasshoppers leap by the dozens into the water, only to drown? The answer is mind-bending parasitic worms, according to David G. Biron of France's National Scientific Research Center. After conducting postmortem examinations on grasshoppers found floating dead in a swimming pool, he and his research group discovered the cause. The larva of a minuscule hairworm, known by the scientific name of *Spinochordodes tellinii*, orchestrates the grasshoppers' suicidal actions by unleashing psychotropic chemicals that urge the insects to take the deadly plunge. It works like this: the larva enters a grasshopper's body, possibly when the insect drinks infested water, and grows there until it is ready to become an adult. At that point, it releases the chemicals, which cause the grasshopper to leap into the water (although it cannot swim) and the worm escapes the dying insect. In the water, the worm finds potential mates, which have likewise abandoned their drowning hosts, and produce the next round of larvae. These survive in the water until the next thirsty grasshopper arrives.

Above left: Described by some cultures as an "old bald-headed man" or a "child of the earth," the Jerusalem cricket lives in the southwestern United States and in Mexico.

Order Hemiptera

With names like toe-biters and water scorpions, these aquatic insects are known for both their physical features and the painful wounds that they can inflict. Toe-biters, also called water bugs, have the appearance of insect body builders. Their bodies are flat, but stocky-looking because they are so wide. Most are oval, but some are almost round. The front pair of legs are bulky above the joint, calling to mind a weight lifter's biceps. The insect typically holds these two claw-tipped legs forward, so that they mimic a pair of enormous jaws. It is the insect's actual mouth, however, that delivers the bite. This insect, and indeed all of the so-called "true bugs" of the order Hemiptera, have mouthparts fashioned into a piercing beak. The water bug's beak is normally tucked away along the lower side of the head, but with lightning speed the bug can use its forelegs to grasp a passerby and flip out its beak to stab the prey, whether it be another insect, a tadpole, a small fish, or a salamander. The needle-sharp beak also injects a substance that subdues and begins to predigest the prey. The water bug then uses the beak to suck out the prey's liquefied innards. Water bugs are also known to stab the toe of a hapless person who wades a bit too close. Although painful, the bite is not dangerous to humans. Many water bugs grow quite large. The giant water bug (*Lethocerus americanus*), common through much of North America, can grow to about 2 inches (5.1 cm) long and an inch (2.5 cm) wide. People usually encounter the insect in ponds or swimming pools, or near an outdoor light. Their penchant for nighttime illumination gives them yet another common name: electric-light bugs. The largest species, found in South America, can reach 4 inches (10.2 cm) long.

Scorpion Look-alikes

Although water scorpions are not really scorpions—scorpions have eight legs and are more closely related to spiders—water scorpions somewhat resemble scorpions. Like the water bug, many water scorpions have wide bodies and often hold their strong, raptorial front legs in front of the head in a posture equivalent to that of a scorpion outstretching its pair of enlarged front legs. Although it lacks the scorpion's

A giant water bug uses its strong forelegs to capture tadpoles and other water creatures, and then finishes the job by impaling the prey on its sharp beak.

foreleg pincers, the water scorpion is still able to hang on to prey animals quite effectively. The two creatures also differ in their methods of defense. The scorpion stings with its tail, and its toxin can cause pain and swelling in a stung person. The water scorpion has a tail-like filament, but it lacks a stinger. Rather, it inflicts a quite painful bite with its piercing mouth in the same manner as the water bug. Some species of water scorpion, especially those in the genus *Ranatra*, are extremely thin and scarcely resemble scorpions. Rather, they are dead ringers for insects called walkingsticks, because both look like slender twigs, until they take a step. These skinny water scorpions hold their forelegs in front of the head just like their stockier peers, but these thin limbs resemble antennae rather than the front legs of a scorpion.

Although its common name is water stick insect, this species *(Ranatra linearis)* is a true bug in the water scorpion family (Nepidae) and is unrelated to the land-living walkingsticks.

SCI-FI MODELS

Science fiction movies are rife with monster insects and monsters based on insects. Children of the 1950s and 1960s are familiar with a series of horror movies starring mutant insects that grew to enormous size. *Mothra* featured a 30-foot-wide (9 m) caterpillar, and in one movie it shared the billing with Godzilla, another enormous animal, although not an insect. In the film *Them!*, towering, man-eating ants took to the screen. Since then, dozens of movies have featured killer bees, locusts, mantids, and other insects. In some, such as *The Fly* (released in 1958 and starring Vincent Price), people take on insect characteristics. In this thriller, a man actually melds with a fly and eventually turns into the insect. As Hollywood began to explore outer space, insects invaded other worlds. In *Starship Troopers*, a 1997 film based loosely on the 1959 book by Robert Heinlein, earthlings battle an alien insect army that threatens the human race. Insects are apparently popular moviegoing fare: The 1986 remake of *The Fly* starring Jeff Goldblum is now a horror classic, and a new version is in the works; the film version of *Starship Troopers* has already spawned a sequel as well as a television series.

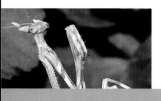

Order Mantodea

Above: A mantid often remains still or moves very slowly . . . until a prey insect happens by. Then, it strikes out with lightning speed, grasping the prey with its powerful front legs.

Right: The Indian rose mantid has an extremely long and thin thorax that separates its front pair of legs from the rear two, giving this clearly non-human creature an eerily human stance.

If ever an animal on Earth appeared to be more suited to an alien world, it would likely be a mantid. These insects, including the well-known praying mantid (sometimes called a praying mantis), have an otherworldly "intelligent" guise. This is probably due to the mantid's head, which unlike almost every other insect's, can cock from one side to the other and gives the impression that it is pondering its next move. Its appearance is enhanced by sizable eyes and substantial front legs, which it often uses for grasping, just as humans use their hands.

Over the Top

Although every member of this group can rightfully be described as bizarre, a few are over the top. One of this number is the wandering violin or Indian rose mantid (*Gongylus gongylodes*), which grows to about 3.1 to 3.9 inches (8–10 cm) long. This insect, with a projection on its head that resembles a tall, thin crown, has a regal air. Its thorax is extremely narrow and long with a widening near the head that looks something akin to a shoulder robe or shawl. Its front legs connect beneath the "robe." The two hind pairs of legs—all even thinner than the thorax—project much farther back on the body, near the short and comparatively wide abdomen. The final touch is a leafy ruffle that covers the bend of the joint midway down each of the rear four legs. Native to parts of Southeast Asia, the wandering violin mantid and its outrageous countenance is popular with insect enthusiasts the world over.

Bright and Bold Mantids

Three other outlandish mantids are the hooded or leaf mantid (*Choeradodis stalii*) of South America, the Madagascan marbled or savannah mantid (*Polyspilota aeruginosa*) of Africa, and the banded flower mantid (*Theopropus elegans*) of Southeast Asia.

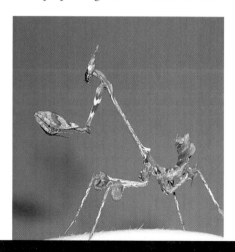

The hooded mantid, which grows to about 5 inches (13 cm) long, is a standout because of its unusual body shape. Its thorax is extended into a pentagon shape that, along with its wide wings, can completely conceal its six legs: the raptorial pair (those that are adapted to seize prey) near the head and the two pair closer to the abdomen.

The marbled mantid, on the other hand, is unusual for its split personality. This 2.4- to 2.8-inch-long (6–7 cm) insect usually remains incognito as it slowly walks about with only its unexceptional brown back showing. When threatened, however, the insect faces its attacker and rears up to show off its red, purple, and/or blue underside. It also fans its wings and outstretches its forelegs, revealing large black spots at the middle joint. Although some insects strike a menacing pose with little to back it up, this species has the characteristically powerful mantid forelegs that it can quickly flick out to ward off many predators.

A bright and bold pattern is the hallmark of the banded flower mantid. This species, sometimes called the elegant mantid, is lime green with a strip of white on its forewings. At rest, when the wings are laid over the abdomen, the white strip resembles a low-slung belt. The thorax and all six legs continue the theme with a white-on-green pattern, clearly evident as regularly spaced white rings around the green legs. It is especially noticeable on the forelegs, which are bulky from the body almost all the way to the claws. As with many mantids, the female banded flower mantid is noticeably larger than the male. He grows to about three-quarters of an inch (2 cm), but she can reach more than twice that size (1.8 inches, or 4.6 cm).

From this angle, the head and folded-up front legs are clearly visible. From the top, however, the widened thorax help this leaf mantid blend into the leaves of the tropical forest where it lives.

Remarkable Beetles

Above: Naturalist Charles Darwin (1809–82) was an avid—if not fanatical —beetle collector. At Cambridge, he had a special six-drawer cabinet built to house his numerous specimens.

Right: The extreme shape of this violin beetle comes from its unusual wings that expand around and frame the abdomen.

While mantids have a vaguely and perhaps a bit unnervingly human manner with their "arms" and swiveling head, beetles are strange because they look decidedly nonhuman, particularly in their mouthparts. An example is Darwin's stag beetle (*Chiasognathus grantii*) of Chile. Like many other members of the stag beetle family, the male has larger—sometimes much larger—jaws. The jaws of the female Darwin's stag beetle are bigger than her head, but those on the male Darwin's stag beetle are simply enormous. Not counting the jaws, the male beetle is about 1.6 to 2 inches (4–5 cm). With the jaws, the length is at least doubled. The size of each jaw is augmented by its shape: long and essentially straight except for an inwardly curved tip. As a result, the top and bottom jaw tips cross over each other. The sheer magnitude of the jaws suggests that the beetle would deliver a fearsome bite, but they are showy rather than strong. Famed naturalist Charles Darwin described the beetle as "bold and pugnacious" in his 1871 book,

The Descent of Man, and Selection in Relation to Sex. In a feat of true bravery, he tested the insect's bite, and wrote: "When threatened, he faces round, opens his great jaws, and at the same time stridulates loudly. But the mandibles were not strong enough to pinch my finger so as to cause actual pain."

Extreme Shapes

A different but also remarkable species goes by the name violin or banjo beetle (*Mormolyce phyllodes*), a tribute to its unexpected body form. With an extremely slender and protracted head and thorax, and wings that expand around the abdomen, the flat insect

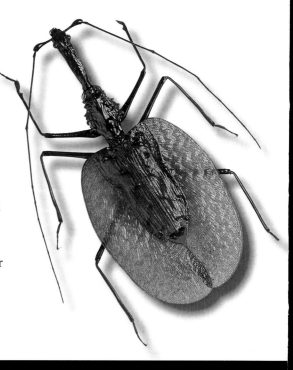

> "One day on tearing off some old bark, I saw two rare beetles and seized one in each hand; then I saw a third and new kind, which I could not bear to lose, so that I popped the one I held in my right hand into my mouth."
>
> —CHARLES DARWIN

resembles these instruments' shapes. The head is perhaps the most distinctive feature with its stretched-out "neck" and thin antennae that are as long as the body. The thorax on this dark brown to black insect is a bit wider than the head, although it is still quite slender, and is decorated with small horny projections. This contrasts with the insect's back end: an abdomen about three times the width of the thorax and framed with kidney-shaped wings that serve to make the rear appear even larger and more circular. This beetle, part of a large family of ground beetles, grows to about 3 inches (7.6 cm) long. Its home is in Sumatra.

Dangerous Larvae

In some instances, the most bizarre beetles are not adults, but their larvae: grubs. One kind that usually gets its share of unflattering adjectives is

SUPER-SIZED INSECTS?

Although some insects can grow to several inches long or have a wingspan of a foot or so, it is impossible for them to attain the mammoth sizes often depicted in horror movies. One reason is that an insect's legs simply could not support the added body weight of increased size. Much of this weight comes from the insect's exoskeleton—the fingernail-like material that encases the body. At the same proportions, a too-large insect would have such a thick and heavy exoskeleton that its legs would buckle under the weight of this mass. The largest known insects ever to traverse the face of the Earth were a species of walkingstick, which reached about 9 inches (22.8 cm) long, and a dragonfly that had a wingspan of about 2.5 feet (76.2 cm). Both have been extinct for millions of years.

the grub of a tiger beetle. Adult tiger beetles, which come in a number of different species, are usually quite handsome, metallic green insects. As grubs, however, they appear more like a maggot with a sickle-jawed beetle head. The larvae of most insects are plant-eaters, but not the tiger beetle grub. This larva burrows underground and then sits in wait at its tunnel entrance. When an insect or other arthropod comes too close, the larva snaps out with its sharp jaws and drags the prey underground to meet its demise. With about 2,000 different species, tiger beetles occur almost worldwide.

Although the six-spotted tiger beetle (*Cicindela sexgutta*) is a striking emerald-toned adult, it was not a beautiful baby. The larva has a maggotlike body with a heavily jawed head.

The Orders Up Close

SPECIFICATIONS

Insects: Grasshoppers, locusts, crickets, katydids

Order: Orthoptera

Meaning of Orthoptera: "straight wing," referring to the shape of the long, thin, leathery forewings

Typical characteristics of adults in this order:

• large hind legs well suited to leaping

• a portion of the thorax, called the pronotum, that is expanded to cover much of the body like a shield

• a slender body, or in the case of katydids, a leaf-shaped one

• two pairs of wings, including a hardened front pair called tegmina, that cover a larger, filmy, folded pair that fan out for flight

• long antennae, although they are short in some species

DIVERSITY

Number of known species: about 21,500

Size: Some of the smallest are the ant crickets (various species of the genus *Mymecophilus*), which have body lengths around 0.08 inches (0.2 cm). The giant bush cricket (*Macrolyristes imperator*) of Malaysia is among the largest members of this order and reaches 4.7 inches (12 cm) or more.

Sampling of benefits to humans: aesthetic value for their calls, drawing people in some cultures to keep them as pets; grasshoppers also occasionally used as human food

The assassin bug, like others in the family Reduviidae, uses its curved beak to pierce its prey and inject a toxin.

SPECIFICATIONS

Insects: Stink bugs, leaf-footed bugs, assassin bugs, water striders, and others

Order: Hemiptera (note: this order is sometimes combined with Homoptera, which include the aphids and cicadas)

Meaning of Hemiptera: "half wing," referring to the forewing, which is thick and leathery on its front half, and thin and membranous on the back half

Typical characteristics of adults in this order:

• two pairs of wings

• relatively short hind wings that are used for flight but are otherwise hidden beneath the forewings

• a piercing beak that points backward beneath the insect

• conspicuous triangular-shaped structure, called a scutellum, on the thorax

DIVERSITY

Number of known species: about 38,000

Size: One of the smaller members of this order is the bedbug, which is about 0.2 inches (0.4–0.6 cm) long. Giant water bugs are some of the largest at 1.5 inches (3.8 cm) in length.

Sampling of benefits to humans: Some are insect predators and help to limit pest species, and many serve as food for other insects, fishes, and birds.

The red-and-black shield on this locust's back is an enlarged pronotum, which is the first section of the thorax. This feature is typical of members in the order Orthoptera.

PARASITIC INSECTS

Called twisted-wings, these tiny insects are astonishing for the way they live. Newly born larvae use their six legs to creep up to and eventually burrow into a grasshopper, wasp, or other insect. Once inside the host's body, the twisted-wing larva undergoes a body rearrangement, losing its legs and its noticeable head, and living off nutrients gleaned from the host's blood and other tissues. For its next trick, the larva pupates and finally emerges as a sexually mature adult. The male adult sprouts wings and leaves the host in search of a mate. Conversely, the female adult remains in the host—mostly. She pokes just enough of her body outside to entice a male. Never seeing her partner, she mates and withdraws back into the host's body, where her young develop inside of her. The next generation of larvae are born live, and exit the host to start the whole process again. Although they are sometimes considered a type of beetle, twisted-wings usually are listed in their own separate order, called Strepsiptera.

SPECIFICATIONS

Insects: Mantids

Order: Mantodea

Meaning of Mantodea: a variation of *mantis*, the historical Greek name for the insect

Typical characteristics of adults in this order:

• outsized forelegs bearing numerous spines

• a triangular-shaped head that the insect can turn from side to side as well as upside down

• two huge eyes and two long, thin antennae

• two pairs of wings

• two small projections, called cerci, at the end of the abdomen

DIVERSITY

Number of known species: more than 1,500

Size: The smallest mantid is known by the scientific name of *Mantoida tenuis* and grows to just 0.4 inches (1 cm) long. In comparison, the largest is an African species, *Ischnomantis gigas*, that reaches 6.7 inches (17 cm) from head to tail end.

Sampling of benefits to humans: predators of many insects, including garden pests

Above: Among the twisted-wings, only the males possess wings. The membranous hind pair are used for flying, while the front pair are tiny and clublike.

Background: When a grasshopper, katydid, or other orthopteran takes flight, its hardened forewings spread wide, and two, larger, previously concealed hind wings fan out.

Below: The spines, evident on the forelegs of this mantid, help the predacious insect to hang on to its prey.

CHAPTER 3

TAKING A CLOSER VIEW

INSECTS SEE, FEEL, AND SMELL; they breathe oxygen; they have blood—the same things that make them so like humans also make them very different. For instance, there are colors that a bee sees as it approaches a flower that are invisible to a person. Smells that drive a moth into a mating frenzy go completely unnoticed by a human. Oxygen that enters a person with a deep breath and travels through the body via the blood instead enters an insect primarily through its abdomen and bypasses the blood completely. Insect blood itself is a different color. Instead of traveling through the body in a never-ending loop of vessels, as it does in humans, insect blood mainly squishes around in the body cavity, providing a liquid pool that bathes the organs and tissues. These contrasts impart much of the alien quality to insects and also make them immensely interesting. Just what are the internal and external characteristics that have allowed them to adapt to conditions on Earth and that set them apart from other creatures?

Left: Flowers often have contrasting ultraviolet patterns, invisible to humans but obvious to the bees and other insects that visit them.
Inset: The male (at left) of this mating pair of cecropia moths no doubt found the female by using his feathery antennae to home in on the pheromones she released when she was ready to take a partner.

Eyes

Vision in humans is considerably dissimilar to vision in insects, although it does essentially the same thing. A person's eye is covered by the cornea, a thin, transparent covering. Inside the eye and toward the front is a lens, a part of which is visible as the pupil. Depending on the amount of light, the colored iris covers more or less of the lens, and the pupil appears smaller or larger, respectively. The lens transmits the incoming light to the retina, a thin tissue made of sensory cells—photoreceptors called rods and cones—on the back of the eye. The retina then uses a pathway in the nervous system to communicate the visual information it has gathered with the brain, and an image forms instantaneously.

A Compound Eye

Although just as immediate, insect vision is not identical to human vision. Each insect eye is actually a collection of eye units, known as ommatidia (the singular is ommatidium). Depending on the species, this compound eye, as it is known, may contain only a few ommatidia or hundreds, thousands, and even tens of thousands. As does the human eye, an ommatidium has a see-through cornea covering its lens and a cluster of photoreceptors deeper inside. With so many ommatidia sending information to the brain, it was first assumed that insects saw multiple, simultaneous pictures of the same image. Scientists now believe that they see a mosaic, like the collection of pixels on a computer screen: each ommatidium views the image, and they all transmit their information to the brain, which combines it into a single picture.

Besides compound eyes, insects often have several smaller eyes, called simple eyes, or ocelli. The ocelli usually are visible as little more than three pinholes that form a small triangle between the compound eyes on an adult insect. They are also present on many larvae. The ocelli do not affect the clarity of the view the insect sees with its compound eyes. Instead, they register the presence or absence of light and make the view brighter or dimmer. Certain insects, such as fleas, have poor eyesight because they lack compound eyes and rely solely on their ocelli.

Motion Detecting

Studies of insect sight suggest that their vision is less crisp than a human's, although some insect species see better than others. They are, however, well-suited to noticing even the tiniest

The compound eyes of the dragonfly are made up of thousands of microscopic units known as ommatidia. Its brain combines the information from all of the units into one image that it instantaneously sees.

"The difficulty of believing that a perfect and complex eye could be formed by natural selection, though insuperable by our imagination, can hardly be considered real."

—CHARLES DARWIN

NIGHTTIME COLORS

Many animals, including humans, see color well during the day, but after the sun sets colors fade to shades of gray and black. This shift from color vision to color blindness occurs in all creatures, except for one. Although a few animal species can still make out colors in low light, scientists are aware of only a single species that can distinguish colors in the dead of night. Studies conducted by Almut Kelber of Sweden's Lund University and his research group revealed that a species of moth, known as the elephant hawk-moth (*Deiliphila elpenor*), can discriminate hues even on a dimly starlit night. The hawkmoths, sleek pink and olive-tan insects from Europe and Asia, put the talent to good use as they navigate between specific-colored flowers to gather nectar at night.

changes in movements just fractions of a second apart. For example, insects in general can continue to track the turning spokes on a wheel long after they become a blur to a human. This skill becomes crystal clear when an annoyed person tries to flick away a fly or a collector tries to net a dragonfly.

Color Vision

Scientists also believe that certain insects have exceptional color vision that extends even into the ultraviolet range. Many of these are insects that feed on the nectar buried inside flowers. The typical butterfly, for example, has a preference for orange and purple flowers. Many flowers do more than display a color; they also provide a road map of sorts that directs the insect to their nectar. This may be accomplished by the petal arrangement or by the addition of ultraviolet color streaks that effectively point to the nectar. Since bees and many other nectar-eating insects can see UV light, which humans cannot, they just follow the signs to their next meal.

Unlike humans and most other animals, which lose their color vision when the light dims, the elephant hawkmoth can distinguish between colors at night.

Insect eyes can track very high-speed movements. While a human sees a continuously moving picture when watching a film, an insect would see a stream of still photos: the images on the film's individual frames.

Spiracles and Respiration

Insect legs are ill suited to carrying a great deal of weight, a fact that limits their size. Another characteristic that precludes insects from becoming too large is the way they breathe.

Humans and other mammals get their oxygen in the same manner: it enters through the nostrils or the mouth, travels down the windpipe to the lungs, where the blood picks it up for delivery to every nook and cranny inside the body, no matter how far distant. Even the largest mammal, the blue whale, obtains all of its oxygen through two nostrils positioned on the top of its head—called blowholes—that carry it into the lungs and out through the blood to its body. As the cells use the oxygen, they give off a waste product, carbon dioxide (two oxygen molecules linked with a carbon molecule), which leaves the body via a reversal of the same route: from the blood to the lungs, up the windpipe, and out of the body.

Insects, on the other hand, use a more direct approach that completely eliminates the lungs, which they do not possess, and the blood. They employ a row of nostril-like openings, not on the head, but running along either side of the thorax and abdomen. These openings are called spiracles.

How Spiracles Work

In a few insects, such as the primitive wingless species, the spiracles remain open constantly. In the vast majority, however, surrounding muscles and

Compared with the overall body size, the legs of this tropical rose chafer (a beetle in the genus *Cetonia*) are rather feeble-looking. Because the insect is small and light, however, the legs are sufficiently strong to not only support it, but also to transport it.

SIZE MATTERS

Ants can lift a great deal of weight compared to their size: 10, 20, even 50 times their body weight. If humans could do the same, a 150-pound (68 kg) person could lift a car or even a bus. Ants and other insects, however, are not exceptionally strong. In fact, if a person were shrunk to ant size, he or she could lift the same seemingly enormous weights. This is because size matters. As an organism becomes smaller, its overall weight drops much more quickly than its strength. The opposite is also true: as an organism gains overall size, its muscle strength increases at a much slower rate. A simple mathematical formula pinpoints the difference: overall weight increases as the cube of body length, while strength increases as the square. In other words, an ant that grew to 100 times its former size would be 10,000 times as strong (100 x 100), but would also weigh 1,000,000 times as much (100 x 100 x 100). Its muscles would be no match for the added weight, let alone picking up a car, too. Math aside, it is still impressive to see a tiny ant haul a much larger wasp across the ground or effortlessly lift a relatively huge leaf above its head.

A colored scanning electron micrograph of a tobacco or warehouse moth caterpillar (*Ephestia elutella*) shows one tiny opening, called a spiracle, in each of the insect's segments. Instead of breathing through the nose as do humans, insects get their air through the spiracles.

flaps control the spiracles in a manner rather like the opening and shutting of the whale's blowholes. Valves on the individual spiracles open inward for inhalation or outward for exhalation. Usually, an insect has two pairs on its thorax and one pair of spiracles on each segment of its abdomen, so the holes are fairly evenly spaced down the body. From the spiracles, the oxygen moves into a network of interconnecting tubes. These tubes transport the oxygen to the different areas of the body. At the ends of the myriad branching tubes, the oxygen crosses into cells and the carbon-dioxide waste product moves from the cells into the tubes for eventual release from the body.

Unlike the mammal's respiratory system, which forcibly pushes blood-borne oxygen to far-reaching body regions, the oxygen in an insect radiates from the spiracles to the cells slowly. Some larger insects help the process along by contracting and relaxing their abdominal muscles while simultaneously opening and closing their spiracles. This creates a bellowslike motion to help draw in and circulate air. Yet, even with the added air movement, the insect system of respiration would be unable to support too large an insect. The expanse from the spiracles to the most distant body regions would simply become too great. The cells would die, and so would the insect.

Antennae

The antennae are one of the most important components of the insect's sensory accoutrements. They help the animal feel, smell, and even taste. With rare exceptions, juvenile and adult insects sport antennae, although they may be reduced to the point that they are imperceptible. They fall into one of two main types. In one, the so-called segmented antennae, muscles along the full length can control the movement of each individual segment, providing a wide range of maneuverability. The other type, called an annulated antennae, has muscles only at the base and the rest of the antennae follows the movement of the base. Insects routinely use their antennae for feeling their way around, tapping them gently against the ground and other objects of interest.

Below: Researchers have only recently discovered exactly how fruit flies use their antennae to smell. Through genetic experiments, they identified 32 odor receptors on each antenna.

SPINNING FILAMENTS

Antennae can help an insect smell and taste, and at least in some flies, it can also help them hear. Researchers Martin Göpfert and Daniel Robert of Switzerland's University of Zurich discovered the unique mechanism behind the feat by carefully observing the antennae of the *Drosophila melanogaster* fruit fly as they subjected them to sound. Each minute antenna has a base that looks like an oblong acorn with a feathery filament protruding. Sound vibrations cause the filament to quiver, which in turn sets the base to spinning. This triggers its sound sensors. Since their finding, the researchers have examined other related flies and found the same type of odd but very functional setup.

A Variety of Styles

The shape and size of the antennae vary widely from one variety of insect to the next. For example, dragon-flies have small, bristly stubs while some longhorn beetles have such fantastically elongated antennae that it appears the insect should tip forward from the weight, but the beetle actually carries them easily. Often, the size and shape of the antennae—whether thin and straight, long and elbowed, comblike, or leafy—help entomologists identify the type of insect and sometimes its sex. The gypsy moth (*Lymantria dispar*) is an example. The female has thin antennae about half as long as her body. The male has antennae of a similar length, but they are feathery and wide.

Pheromones

The variance in size and shape of the gypsy moth's antennae highlights one of their sensory uses: smell. Gypsy moths, harmful pests of hardwood trees, are forest creatures that emerge from their pupae for about a week of mating before they die. In that short time frame, a male has to find a female in the often-thick vegetation of the forests where they live. To make

"We hope that, when the insects take over the world,
they will remember with gratitude how we took them along on all our picnics."

—RICHARD VAUGHAN

matters worse, the female cannot fly, even though she has a 2-inch (5.1 cm) wingspan. Fortunately, she has another tactic. She releases a scent, called a pheromone. The male's plumose antennae are laden with highly sensitive receptors that can pick up trace amounts of the pheromone among the other diverse scents in the woods and follow the slight scent to the waiting female. In fact, males are so good at tracking the scent that humans have begun using pheromone-laced traps to lure and to capture male gypsy moths in an attempt to control their populations.

Following the Scent

An antenna's sense of smell is not limited to pheromones. Honey bees and many other pollinating insects follow the scent of flowers, while others, such as fruit flies, are partial to odors such as ripe or rotting fruit. A study of fruit flies at Yale University reported that each antenna on this minuscule insect has a full 32 odor receptors. For another pesky insect, the oak bark beetle (a group of species in the genus *Pseudopityophthorus*), a particular kind of fungus is the alluring odor. The fungus is known as oak wilt fungus, because it infects oak trees and causes their leaves to wilt. The trees die soon thereafter. The fungus reproduces beneath the bark and eventually breaks through, drawing oak bark beetles. The beetles lay their eggs under the bark and amid the fungus and then fly off, inadvertently carrying spores of the fungus on their bodies. They spread the fungus when they land on another healthy oak tree.

A Sense of Taste

Besides touch and smell, some insects may use their antennae to taste things in their paths. Although most insects do their tasting with their mouths, ants, bees, and wasps all have taste receptors on their antennae, too, so they can not only feel an object, but also determine if it is edible.

Far left: From one species to the next, insect antennae come in a variety of shapes. This long-horned beetle from Southeast Asia has thin, segmented feelers.

Below: A red fire ant can ensure that another ant is part of its clan with a brush of its antennae. If it is not, the fire ant can stir its nest mates to attack the trespasser.

INSECT IDENTIFIERS

A common sight at a picnic is a row of ants marching to and from a dropped ice cream cone or other food source. But ants can use their antennae to do more than find the next meal. They can also lay their feelers on another ant to determine whether it is a part of their colony. Among red fire ants (*Solenopsis invicta*), the discovery of an interloper triggers a swift and deadly attack. Scientist James Anderson of the University of Mississippi is hoping to learn more about the identification skills of the ants, which have spread from their native South America to the United States, where they cause billions of dollars in crop and other damage every year. He and his research group have confirmed that the ants smear themselves and their nest mates with a chemical substance that makes them recognizable to one another. With additional studies, he hopes to learn how to disrupt their identification skills and trigger the ants in a colony to mistake their nest mates for intruders and therefore control their own population.

Ovipositors and Cerci

Female ichneumon wasps, such as this one, have extremely long ovipositors for drilling into dead, standing trees and laying their eggs inside.

Insects have jaws, so it is not surprising that the larger insects can take a pretty good nip at a curious person's prodding finger. A number of smaller insects can also inflict some pain, but most do so with a stinger rather than their mouths. Bees, hornets, and wasps are known for their stings, but it is only the females that are the culprits. This is because the stinger is really a modified egg-laying structure, called an ovipositor, which literally means "egg placer."

The Ovipositor

The females of many other non-stinging insects also have noticeable ovipositors, which they use to place their eggs in favorable locations, perhaps within a leaf or a rotting log, or to bury them in the sand. Frequently, the ovipositor is so pronounced that it provides a quick and easy way to tell a female from a male. In many grasshoppers and katydids, for example, the female's ovipositor looks like a spike protruding from the tip of her abdomen. The female greater arid-land katydid (*Neobarrettia spinosa*) has an ovipositor that rivals her body in length. Female ichneumon wasps have some of the longest ovipositors in the insect world. The female giant ichneumon (*Megarhyssa atrata*) has a body that can reach 1 to 1.5 inches (2.5–3.8 cm) long and an ovipositor that extends 2 to 5 inches (5.1–12.7 cm) farther. Despite the alarming appearance of the female's ovipositor, only a few species of ichneumons sting. Most, including the giant ichneumon, are harmless and use the ungainly ovipositor solely to drill into dead, standing trees, where they lay their eggs near or sometimes in the bodies of wood-boring grubs or maggots. When the eggs hatch, the larvae feast on these soft-bodied prey.

The Cerci

Many insects appear to have a pair of tails on the back end of the abdomen. These appendages have the role of rear feelers and are called the cerci (the singular is cercus). Depending on the species, the cerci may be tiny or absent altogether, or they may be quite conspicuous. Examples of insects with large cerci include earwigs and mayflies. Earwigs, often seen scurrying for dark and damp cover when a rock or rotting log is overturned, typically have thick, pincerlike cerci. One of the most well-known earwigs is the common earwig (*Forficula auricularia*), a native of Europe but now spread throughout much of the world, sometimes including people's homes. Both the males and females of this species have cerci, but the males' are twice as long as the females' and curved rather than straight.

Mayflies, too, have large cerci, but the insects little resemble earwigs. Mayflies are slender-bodied creatures with four wings and spend their very short adult life spans flitting about, usually within a few hundred yards of water, in search of a mate. Their two cerci are threadlike and long, sometimes as long as the body. A number of them, including the western green drake (*Drunella grandis*), also have a third, similarly sized "tail" between the two cerci. This is known as a caudal filament. Even the larva of this species, which lives in lakes and other bodies of freshwater, has the two cerci and the tail filament. When it crawls onto land, its back splits open and the winged form emerges for its brief day or two in the sun.

The common earwig has two pincerlike cerci. Females, such as the one pictured here, have fairly straight cerci, while males' cerci are curved strongly inward.

SURVIVAL SPECIALISTS

Caterpillars poop—a lot. Tearing into the silken nest of the eastern tent caterpillar (*Malacosoma americanum*), a common North American species, will release such a stockpile of frass, as it is called, that is difficult to imagine how the caterpillars fit in the nest with it. Not all caterpillars wallow in their own waste, however. The larvae of a little butterfly called the silver-spotted skipper (*Epargyreus clarus*) does not just defecate; it blasts its frass up to 5 feet (152 cm) away. Researcher Martha Weiss of Georgetown University in Washington, D.C., studied the caterpillars to find out why they fired their feces such a distance. By manually retrieving the waste pellets and placing them near the caterpillars, she discovered that the flinging of the frass helped protect the larvae from a kind of wasp that keys in on the waste pellets to find caterpillar prey. In other words, the caterpillar was not just a neat freak after all, but rather a survival specialist.

This caterpillar of the silver-spotted skipper has a bizarre behavior: it fires its waste pellets up to an astonishing 5 feet (152 cm) away.

The Circulatory System

This dragonfly, which has just emerged from its life in the water as a larva, is still perched on top of its old exoskeleton. Its new wings inflate to full size with the help of blood that flows into their veins.

Although an insect's blood does not carry oxygen, it does perform the other functions that a human's blood does. It collects nutrients from digested food and ferries them to the cells, which use them as an energy source. It transports hormones, which control all sorts of bodily functions, including reproduction and growth. It helps in the fight against bacteria and other invaders. In many insects, it helps warm or cool the insect by transferring heat between the core of the body and areas closer to the surface. Another quality the insect's blood shares with that of humans is that it is a liquid made mostly of water. Because insect blood does not have the hemoglobin that carries oxygen in human blood, however, it is not red. As any driver or passenger can attest, insect blood is yellow to greenish, even after it has dried on a car windshield.

An Open System

One of the greatest differences between the circulatory system of humans and insects is the way the blood moves. A human's blood traverses the body inside vessels, while much of an insect's blood just sloshes around inside the body, literally bathing the organs and tissues. This is called an open circulatory system, because the blood is not always constrained in vessels. If the blood were fully contained,

Unlike the circulatory system in a human body, the blood in an insect only periodically enters vessels. During the rest of the time, it floats freely inside the body cavity.

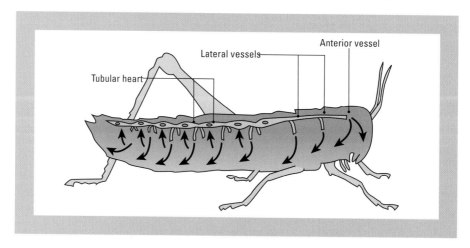

Tubular heart

Lateral vessels

Anterior vessel

as it is in humans and other typical vertebrates, it would be known as a closed circulatory system.

Insects are not completely without blood vessels. They even have a heart, although it shares little in common with the fist-sized organ found in humans. The insect heart is located in the abdomen and is a short, pulsing piece of a blood vessel that runs down the back. Muscles along the vessel pump blood from the abdomen forward, forcing blood through one-way valves from one vessel chamber to the next, until it eventually spills out into the head, where it oozes around the brain. Depending on the insect's species, its size, and its individual activity level, the heart muscles may contract a few dozen to a couple of hundred times each minute. The outside temperature can also slow or speed the heartbeat. Because insects are cold-blooded, their muscles work faster on a warm day and more slowly on a chillier one.

Making a Transition

Once in the head, the blood meanders back through the body, eventually winding up in the abdomen for another circuit to the head. Once the blood is outside of the vessel, its journey through the body is driven by the individual insect's movements. Wing-flapping, walking, lifting, and even breathing exerts pressures that swish the blood to and fro. One place that blood may flow is into the scaffolding, or veins, that are evident within an insect's wing. This is perhaps best witnessed in dragonflies as they make their transition from unwinged larva to adult. The larva crawls out of the water where it has lived for many months, its back splits open, and the new adult slowly arises. Still crushed against the body, the wings begin to inflate to their full size as blood slips into the veins. The complete transformation may take an hour or so, but to a patient observer, the show is remarkable.

The hemlock borer (*Melanophila fulvoguttata*) is one of several species that will lay their eggs in diseased or fire-damaged trees. This larva is revealed under the bark of a mature, recently killed eastern hemlock tree.

THE REAL FIREBUGS

Arsonists are known as firebugs, but the term could easily apply to certain types of beetles that flock to the still-smoldering sites of forest fires. There, the wood-boring beetles (species of the genus *Merimna* and the genus *Melanophila*) mate and lay their eggs, and the hatchlings feed on the wood of dead trees. Amazingly, the adult beetles can sense a forest fire from miles away. They do it through smoke and heat detectors located on their bodies. The *Melanophila* beetles use smoke detectors on their antennae and heat sensors on the thorax to pinpoint the blaze. The *Merimna* beetles have infrared (heat) sensors on the abdomen. The heat sensors have piqued the interest of the U.S. military, which is now funding studies of the insects to find out whether they may lead to improvements in current infrared technology or perhaps provide a way to lessen the costs of currently used heat-sensing equipment.

INSECTS UNDERCOVER

PART 2

CHAPTER 4

SPECTACULAR CAMOUFLAGE

INSECT PREDATORS ARE MANY. To a grasshopper, for example, birds flying overhead, frogs waiting in ambush on a pond's shoreline, snakes slithering stealthily through meadow grass, and rodents busily scurrying along the forest edge all pose threats. It is not surprising, then, that insects have developed a number of tactics to help them avoid capture. One of the most effective is camouflage. Many insects have body shapes or colors that help them blend into the background; they essentially disappear from their foe's sight. Insects that look like stems, leaves, thorns, and bark fool all but the most careful observers, and that includes humans. Their illusions are a good example of how evolution works. Individuals that have the best camouflage are apt to survive longer than those more obvious to predators, and many of these individuals then go on to produce a greater number of young. If the young inherit the advantageous trait—the camouflage—they also are well-disguised and later have young similarly and sometimes better endowed. Eventually, best-concealed individuals make up an ever-expanding portion of the population, and the species evolves to become increasingly elusive.

Left: The first segment of the thorax of the thorn bug *Umbonia crassicornis* rises sail-like above its back in a convincing replica of a thorn. Inset: This stick insect, *Ctenomorpha chronus*, might easily be mistaken for a twig or small branch—but not as a tasty morsel—by a passing bird. Pages 42–43: A praying mantid is easily overlooked when perched within the branches of similarly colored shrubbery.

Stick Mimics

The camouflage of walkingsticks and leaf insects is amazing. Although some can grow to 6 inches (15 cm) long or more, they are such excellent mimics of bare and leafy twigs and stems that they can remain hidden from sight even on close inspection.

Walkingsticks

The typical walkingstick has an appearance just as its name implies: it looks like a slender, leafless stick that has sprouted thin, delicate legs. Its legs spread out over an extremely elongated thorax, so that the second and third pairs of legs occur at about one-third and two-thirds of the way down the body. The insect usually walks with these four legs, holding the remaining two legs, which connect just behind the head, out in front like another set of antennae. The body is frequently a near-identical diameter and color, and sometimes about the same texture, as the stem or twig on which the insect is usually found.

This is true of the giant walkingstick (*Megaphasma dentricus*). It has a slender, green-brown body that blends well with the branches of wild cherry and other trees where it

spends most of the day. A resident of the southern United States, it moves its long, thin legs very slowly, as do other walkingsticks, thus drawing little attention to itself and allowing it to hide in plain sight. Occasionally, a gardener or other outdoor enthusiast will spot a giant walkingstick and snap its picture, only to discover later that he or she has actually photographed two: a mating pair comprising a large female and a much smaller, previously unseen male on her back.

Leaf Insects

Like the walkingsticks, leaf insects are plant eaters and take unhurried steps along branches. As their name suggests, they resemble leaves, or more accurately, leafy sticks. One of the oddest is the 3.5- to 5.5-inch-long (9–14 cm) spiny leaf insect or giant prickly leaf insect (*Extatosoma tiaratum*) of Australia and

Top right: The earthy hue and mottled pattern of the prickly stick insect, *Extatosoma tiaratum*, exactly mimic a bed of fallen leaves; its legs even have leaflike contours to complete the illusion.

Below: With its needlelike body and delicate legs, a walkingstick insect viewed in its chosen habitat makes an observer wonder: "Where does the stick end and the insect begin?"

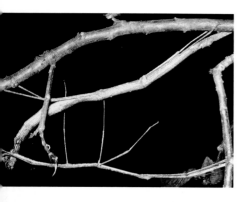

"Of what use, however, is a general certainty that an insect will not walk with his head hindmost, when what you need to know is the play of inward stimulus that sends him hither and thither in a network of possible paths?"

—George Eliot

New Guinea. This species is the image of a dead, curled-up leaf. Tan and brown, it has the same long form of a walkingstick, but its body is wider and its legs are not delicate and slender, but instead spread into leaflike shapes. It sports a number of small spines on the back of its head and here and there along its body, and it generally holds its abdomen in an upward curve. This insect, as well as many other members of the order, engages in a behavior that adds to its deception. When a breeze stirs, it not only sways with the stem it is grasping, but it also flexes its legs in a manner that keeps the insect in concert with the movements of the plant and does not betray its true identity.

Sacrificial Legs

Despite their cryptic physical and behavioral attributes, walkingsticks and leaf insects both sometimes tangle with predators. Yet, amazingly, some of these insects manage to survive potentially deadly encounters by sacrificing a limb to the predator— and replacing it with a new one. This limb regeneration, rare among insects as well as other animals, occurs among the juveniles of certain species in the order Phasmida. As the immature insect rapidly grows, its old outer skin, or cuticle, splits during a molting process. The lucky juveniles are able to regenerate the missing limb at the next molt.

SPECIFICATIONS

Insects: Walkingsticks and leaf insects

Order: Phasmida (or Phasmatodea)

Meaning of Phasmida: "apparition" or "phantom," apparently referring to their ability to seemingly disappear into a background of twigs and leaves

Typical characteristics of adults in this order:
- usually a long and thin body that may resemble a stick or leaf, until it moves
- two pairs of wings, if present, but many, including most in North America, are wingless
- long, threadlike antennae
- chewing mouthparts
- eggs that hatch into nymphs with an appearance much like miniature adults

DIVERSITY

Number of known species: about 3,000

Size: The smallest species can measure less than 0.04 inches (10 mm) long. The largest is the appropriately named giant walkingstick, *Phobaeticus serratipes*, of the Malay Peninsula. The body of the female, the larger sex, can reach 9 to 14 inches (22.9–36 cm) long. With its legs stretched to the front and rear, the length doubles.

Sampling of benefits to humans: Walkingsticks and leaf insects are common in the pet trade. Some companies also sell the mounted or otherwise preserved insects for wall and desk decoration.

Here, a green walkingstick of the Ecuadorian jungle can be clearly seen in profile, even though to a predator passing overhead its coloring would blend exactly with the green leaf on which it rests.

Thorns, Buds, and Bark

Gardeners are often reminded of insect guise after snipping a handful of wildflowers to arrange in a vase indoors. Almost always, some little creature ambles away from a petal or off a stem and finally makes its presence known. Treehoppers are one of the more unusual insects that sometimes make the transit indoors on just-picked bouquets. Decorative sticks collected from a woodlot are not immune to hitchhikers either and may carry flat bugs and other uninvited guests.

Treehoppers

Treehoppers are interesting for their strange shapes. Some species look like thorns and others like plant buds, providing them with a hard-to-beat cover. One of the larger treehoppers is the buffalo treehopper (*Stictocephala bisonia*), which is all of three-eighths of an inch

(1 cm) long. For its small body size, this species has large yellow-and-black eyes, but its unusually tall thorax is its most memorable feature. The lime-hued thorax—technically the pronotum, which is a plate on the upper surface of the three-segmented thorax—rises sharply to a narrow peak and stretches back to form a roof over the abdomen and forward to cover the head, where it ends in a thornlike point. Although the comparison is a bit strained, the heightened pronotum gives the treehopper a silhouette somewhat like a buffalo with its shoulder hump, and leads to the insect's common name. Transparent wings, readily seen below the pronotum, extend beyond the light-green abdomen. The similar-looking, although wingless juveniles, called nymphs, prefer smaller plants to the adults' trees, but both give the impression of thorns or buds, and not insects. Buffalo treehoppers live in

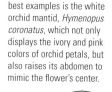

Although few insects mimic flowers, one of the best examples is the white orchid mantid, *Hymenopus coronatus*, which not only displays the ivory and pink colors of orchid petals, but also raises its abdomen to mimic the flower's center.

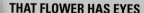

THAT FLOWER HAS EYES

Although many insects mimic leaves, twigs, or other plant parts, only a few are the embodiment of a flower. One of the best flower imitators is the white orchid mantid (*Hymenopus coronatus*) of Southeast Asia. Small enough to sit on the tip of a finger, this ivory insect is tinged with pink, just like the orchid flowers on which it is often found. It has a sharp-featured face that comes to a point above each eye and at the end of the snout. The most flowery features, however, are the legs and abdomen. The insect positions itself with its abdomen curled upward in a near-perfect copy of a flower's central structure, and the elegant pink petal-matching frills on both pairs of hind legs complete the subterfuge.

many areas of the United States, as well as southern Canada.

In some treehoppers, the pronotum is especially tall. The thorn bug (*Umbonia crassicornis*) is a treehopper with such a characteristic. The size and shape of the pronotum varies among individuals, and the so-called horn of the male may rise a full body's length above the back, where it either comes to a point or flattens into a blade shape. Adults, usually yellowish green with brown or red markings, grow to about the same size as buffalo treehoppers. They are found throughout the warmer regions of the New World.

WHAT IS THAT?

Neither walkingsticks nor mantids, although they have some characteristics of each, a new group of insects turned the scientific world on its ear when it was named into its own, brand-new order in 2002. Called heelwalkers, these insects are now classified in the order Mantophasmatodea, a name that combines the orders for mantids (Mantodea) and for walkingsticks (Phasmatodea). A heelwalker has a long, thin body, but it is not quite as slender as a typical walkingstick; and it has the triangular head and predaceous habits of a mantid, but no wings. Growing only to about an inch long (2–3 cm), the insects had been present in museum collections for decades, although often misidentified as juvenile mantids and never specified as a unique order. Since their identity has been made known, scientists have recognized several species in southern Africa.

Flat Bugs

These insects, which are related to water striders and water bugs, are terrestrial insects that make their living on or often within the bark of dead trees. Many species have a mottled pattern of blacks and browns that, even when any covering layer of bark is removed and they are exposed, is nearly impossible to see against the background color and texture. One common species in the southern United States is all black. Known simply as a flat bug (*Aradus gracilicornis*), it is a perfect match for one of its preferred stomping grounds: fire-charred pine trees. Hundreds of the insects, which grow to only a fifth of an inch (4.8–5.8 mm) long, may exist on one burned tree.

The humplike protrusion that lends the buffalo treehopper its name is actually the insect's thorax, which forms a peak over its head and abdomen and ends in a thornlike tip.

Leaf Imitators

A variety of insects come in leaf-like versions, but two groups in particular contain species that are especially adept copycats. One is the katydids, which along with grasshoppers and crickets are part of the order Orthoptera. The other comprises some lineages of the brush-footed butterflies, named for their short, hairy front legs. They are in the family Nymphalidae.

Katydids

Katydids, also called bushcrickets in some parts of the world, hide among aboveground vegetation when they are inactive. To avoid predators that would be happy to make lunch of them, many have evolved remarkably cryptic patterns on their large wings to conceal them from view. Some, such as the leaf katydid (*Aegimia elongata*) of Central America and the broad-winged bush katydid (*Scudderia pistillata*) of the northern United States and southern Canada, sport more than just the emerald green of the nearby leaves. Their wings include a pattern that apes the web of veins on the leaves. The same vein duplication holds true for many other species of katydids, including the oblong-winged katydid (*Amblycorypha oblongifolia*), which is also found in North America. Individuals in this species may be yellow, green, orangish yellow, and occasionally fuchsia, an unusual color in the animal world.

Not all katydids resemble healthy, whole leaves. The common name of the dead-leaf mimetica (*Mimetica mortuifolia*) says it all. This species, often with at least some brown coloration, has irregular-shaped wings that look for all the world like a partially eaten dead leaf. Scientists believe many other species of katydids lurk in the meadows and forests of Earth, but the insects' camouflage, nocturnal habits, and preference for heights has rendered them too elusive for even the keenest-eyed human explorers.

Brush-footed Butterflies

On first glance, it is difficult to believe that some of the brush-footed butterflies could be considered even vaguely cryptic . . . that is, until they close their

Below: Katydids have mastered the art of mimicking foliage in all of its shapes and colors, including dead, tattered, and shiny new leaves. The dead leaf katydid completes its ruse by hanging below a branch.

Background: A leaf nymph, *Kallima paralekta*, displays the bright colors that belie an effective camouflage when its wings are folded.

wings. The leaf nymph (*Kallima paralekta*) is a case in point. When seen from above with its wings spread to their 2.8-to-3.1-inch-wide (7–8 cm) span, midnight blue floods the hind pair and the lower half of the front pair, while the upper half of the forewings is separated into wide shocks of orange and black. Usually, however, this Indonesian butterfly rests with its wings held together, revealing only their lower sides and their exquisite camouflage. Each forewing and hind wing is tan with a lone, narrow, dark stripe running down the center. At rest, the butterfly moves each front and back wing into a position that is the spitting image of a leaf. Even the stripes align to copy a leaf's single, main vein. A few

brush-footed butterflies blend into their environment not by matching its colors, but by letting them show through. One of these is a glasswing butterfly (*Acraea andromacha*), which has a wingspan of about 2.4 inches (6 cm). Its wings are transparent, disrupted only here and there by dark blotches. No matter where this Australian insect lands, it fits right in.

Above: The glasswing butterfly's transparent wings help it blend into any environment.

Below: Although not exactly camouflaged, the milkweed beetle has a secret weapon—its diet of milkweed leaves leave the beetle with a bad taste.

SHOWOFFS

With its basic red color, the half-inch-long (1.3 cm) milkweed beetle (*Tetraopes tetrophthalmus*) brazenly sits out in broad daylight, seemingly inviting a bird to swoop down and gobble it up. Birds, however, regularly ignore the insect. Why? The beetles eat milkweed plants, which contain chemicals similar to the human heart drug digitalis. The chemicals accumulate in the beetle's body and put a bad taste in the mouth of any bird that eats one. To the beetle's benefit, a bird's first experience with a milkweed beetle is usually its last, because it remembers to avoid this and often other red- or orange-hued insects. Scientists call the warning sign aposematic coloration. In most instances, insects that are active during the day and have standout colors or patterns are distasteful, toxic, or otherwise dangerous to would-be predators. For example, many ladybird beetles, also known as ladybugs, are foul-tasting and red in color; the zebra longwing (*Heliconius charitonius*) of the southern United States and many other brush-footed butterflies are similarly nauseating to predators and wear vivid wing patterns; and a variety of stinging insects, such as yellow jackets and bumblebees, are boldly striped in yellow and black.

Protective Coloration

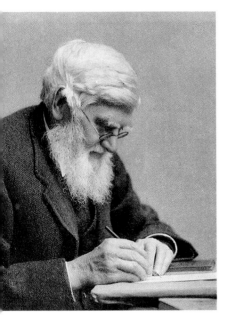

Alfred Russel Wallace, a peer of Charles Darwin, was one of the earliest proponents of natural selection as the mechanism of evolution.

In horse-racing circles, breeders choose the fastest and strongest horses for mating so that they will produce the next generation of winning animal athletes. This is artificial selection: humans breeding organisms to possess certain traits. In natural selection, the choices are just that—natural ones. The animals best able to survive in their surroundings and reproduce successfully have the most young. If those young inherit the favorable traits of their parents, they are more apt to be successful reproducers, too, setting up a path for the trait to become progressively common in the species from generation to generation. Natural selection, then, is the mechanism of evolution in this group.

For years, biology textbooks from around the world have used a certain insect and its camouflage to help explain the concept of natural selection. That insect is the peppered moth (*Biston betularia*), which is found over much of the Northern Hemisphere.

Peppered Moths

Just as humans express variation among individuals—skin, hair, or eye color, for example—many animals have more than one general appearance. The peppered moth has two basic color variants, or morphs. One is ivory with black specks and blotches, giving the moth its "peppered" name; and the second morph is all dark, or melanistic. In addition, hybrids of the two fall somewhere in between.

Until the mid-1800s, the moths were only known from their "peppered" morph. At that point, the melanistic form appeared and over the next decades became increasingly prevalent. At about the same time, the scientific community was looking for modern-day examples to substantiate and explain the idea that natural selection is the mechanism

"I approach with caution, but before I can reach him, *whizz!*—
he is off, and flies humming round my head."

—ALFRED RUSSEL WALLACE, ON COLLECTING INSECTS

of evolution, as proposed by Charles Darwin and Alfred Russel Wallace, who had presented papers outlining their work to the Linnean Society of London in 1858. To many scientists, the rise of the melanistic morph was a perfect living example of the concept. The Industrial Revolution, they hypothesized, had spewed so much pollution into the air that it had darkened the trees enough to affect the moths' survival. In polluted areas, they suggested, melanistic moths could blend in better with the now-darker trees and avoid predation by birds, while the lighter moths became easy targets for predators. This notion would eventually have evidence to back it up, but it would not come until the middle of the twentieth century.

The Classic Study

In experiments conducted in the 1950s, British naturalist and physician Bernard Kettlewell set out to determine whether birds indeed preyed mainly on lighter moths in polluted forests, and whether the opposite was also true. He put identifying marks on both light and dark moths and released them into polluted and unpolluted woodlands. Upon monitoring the moths, he concluded that light moths resting on the dark bark of a tree trunk, and dark moths on light bark, were falling prey to birds more often than their counterparts. Although recent research indicates that Kettlewell's methods were possibly flawed and parts of his conclusions are not supported, his main point that variation in industrial pollution produces variation in melanism with more polluted areas having more melanistic moths is valid. Since Kettlewell's work, and through the numerous studies that have verified it thereafter, peppered moths have become one of the most common examples of natural selection used in biology textbooks. Photographs showing the different morphs of the moths on dark and light bark not only provide a current example of this important biological concept, but also serve as illustrations of the importance of camouflage to an insect's survival.

Above: The peppered moth is a real textbook case—its gradual change in coloration from light to dark as world pollution increased has been used in classrooms for decades to explain natural selection.

Opposite: This darker morph of the peppered moth is better able to blend in with soot-darkened tree trunks; paler morphs are more at risk from predators.

CHAPTER 5

MISTAKEN IDENTITIES

THE SMALL GREEN LACEWING (*Chrysopa slossonaee*) has an unusual story. In eastern Canada and the eastern United States, its diet includes woolly alder aphids (*Prociphilus tesselatus*). The aphids are "woolly" because they secrete waxy fibers that form fuzzy coats over their bodies. A lacewing would find these aphids to be easy pickings, except that the aphids have bodyguards. Ants tend the aphids so that they can lap up a sweet substance, called honeydew, that the aphids produce. The ants very successfully attack other insects that come too close to their aphid herd. Still, they are no match for the lacewing. The immature larva of this insect plucks clumps of the waxy fibers from the aphids' coats, covers its body with the fuzz, and successfully masquerades as a woolly aphid. With this clever costume, the lacewing larva escapes notice from the ants while munching on aphids. The charade not only protects the lacewing, but it nourishes it as well.

Lacewings are not the only insects to survive attack from predators by taking on the appearance of other animals. These include butterflies that would be tasty morsels but avoid consumption because they look like unpalatable species, as well as harmless flies and other insects that are close to mirror images of stinging wasps and bees.

Left: The wingless immature larva of the green lacewing disguises itself to resemble a woolly alder aphid, allowing it to munch on the tiny insects and avoid attack by the aphids' ant guardians.
Inset: Milkweed may be the monarch butterfly's favorite food, but a chemical in the leaves gives the butterfly a nasty taste, making it unpalatable to most birds.

Butterfly Ploys

It makes sense. If a certain species of insect tastes bad to predators, and its appearance wards off future attacks, other species would benefit if they could copy at least those features that repel the attackers. This kind of mimicry is common among butterflies. The resulting similarity between some species can ensure their survival, but can be immensely frustrating for budding human lepidopterists who are trying to figure out which species has touched down on the windowsill.

Below: When tiger swallowtails, which are normally yellow winged with black stripes, flock near blue-and-black pipevine swallowtails, the females often morph into a darker hue to mimic the noxious-tasting pipevine butterflies.

Below right: The viceroy was once thought to mimic the distasteful monarch butterfly, thus gaining its immunity from bird attacks. Recent research has shown that the viceroy has its own unique bad taste.

Tiger Swallowtails and Pipevine Swallowtails

Tiger swallowtails (*Papilio glaucus)* live throughout much of North America, extending as far north as Alaska. Usually, they have yellow wings with black stripes. In some places, however, many of the female tigers are black and blue instead. The presence of another black-and-blue butterfly, the pipevine swallowtail (*Battus philenor*), accounts for the coloration shift. The pipevine eats the leaves of plants that contain noxious chemicals, takes up some of the chemicals into its own body, and becomes distasteful to predators. If they live in the company of the pipevines, the darker tigers can benefit by looking like the distasteful species. And they do: where the two live together, a greater proportion of female tiger swallowtails have the black-and-blue coloration.

Monarchs and Viceroys

Viceroys (*Limenitis archippus*) and monarchs (*Danaus plexippus*) look a lot alike, too. Both are large butterflies with orange wings webbed with black veins and white-spotted, black borders. The viceroy is a bit smaller, with a wingspan of about 2.5 to 3 inches (6.4–7.6 cm), and has an extra black line on its hind wing, but is otherwise almost identical to the monarch. For many years, biology textbooks hyped the pairing as a tasty species copying the appearance of a noxious one, thereby gaining protection, however unearned, from predators. New studies performed in the 1990s, however, revealed that both species are distasteful to their common attackers, birds. So what is going on? Scientists now believe that the two benefit by mimicking each other, thus reaffirming the connection between their appearance and their poor palatability to their would-be predators. This type of mimicry, in which both species are noxious and share a similar warning coloration, is called Müllerian mimicry. In Batesian mimicry, only the model is unpalatable.

Copycat Supreme

Heliconius erato is a butterfly with a number of common names. Why? Because it looks wildly different in different places. In one area, for instance, it sports a brilliant scarlet patch on its forewing and an ivory stripe on the hind wing. A distance away, it may be all black except for two white-and-red spots on each front wing. No matter where it goes, however, it is likely to run into a near-mirror image of itself in the variants of another species,

often called the postman (*Heliconius melpomene*). James Mallet of University College in London is studying the two species and others to determine why wide differences within a species sometimes cause it to split into two or more new species and sometimes do not. The confusingly similar butterflies have also spurred him to investigate just which of the look-alikes are actually the models and which are the copiers.

As a master of insect disguise, this *Heliconius erato* butterfly has acquired a number of common names. Depending on where it lives, it mimics local varients of the butterfly *Heliconius melpornene*.

DISGUSTING DISGUISE

Any child who has ever felt like an ugly duckling can take heart from these caterpillars: they look like bird droppings, but later blossom into lovely moths. One is Harris's three-spot (*Harrisimemna trisignata*). As a caterpillar, it is a close copy of a gob of fresh, shiny, white-and-black-streaked bird poop. When the caterpillar metamorphoses into an adult, however, it becomes a handsome specimen with three reddish-brown dots on its mottled black-and-white forewings, a similarly patterned body, and alabaster hind wings. The moth, which has a 1.2- to 1.4-inch (3–3.6 cm) wingspan, is a North American species.

Although as a larva the Harris's three-spot caterpillar looks like nothing so much as a streak of bird poop, it will soon turn into a handsome black-and-white moth.

Disguised Flies

Look closely at the next bee you spot pollinating a flower or stopping on the edge of a soft drink–filled glass. If all of its wings are visible and it has only two, that "bee" is not a bee at all. A variety of flies, which have only one pair of visible wings, look like bees or other stinging insects and no doubt avoid many an encounter with a predator because of their threatening appearance.

Above right: The bee flies, which form one of the largest families of flies, are amazing mimics. Some, such as this greater bee fly, *Bombylius major*, copy the appearance of its namesake even down to the short hairs on its body.

Below: The yellowjacket hover fly closely resembles the infamous picnic hornet—complete with a narrow wasp waist.

Bee Duplicates

An entire family of flies is so similar to bees that its collective common name is the bee flies. The family, called Bombyliidae, is one of the largest among the flies, with approximately 4,500 species. Some, such as the dark-edged, or greater, bee fly (*Bombylius major*), have short hairs on their bodies, just as many bees do. This species, which is familiar through much of the Northern Hemisphere, is yellow to yellowish-brown and grows to 0.5 to 0.7 inches (1.2–1.8 cm) long. It has a swift, darting flight until it reaches a flower. There, it can hover in place while using its long, thin proboscis to slurp up nectar. Other bee flies

display the stripes typical of many bees. This is evident in species of the genus *Villa*, many of which have abdomens with alternating dark and light bands. As well as two rather than four wings, another feature that distinguishes these bee flies from similar-looking bees is the size of their eyes. A bee fly's two enormous compound eyes are akin to a giant pair of earmuffs squeezed up against one another, covering the head almost completely. A bee's eyes are typically much smaller, and the two do not touch.

Wasp and Hornet Copies

The family Syrphidae includes several flies that appear to be wasps. Many, such as those in the genus *Temnostoma*, have the prominent thorax and abdomen markings and the elongate, brown-tinged wings common to numerous wasps. Another species is so like a yellow jacket hornet that its name is the yellowjacket hover fly (*Milesia virginiensis*). This fly has a lovely yellow, black, and reddish-brown pattern on its abdomen, and black and yellow bars on its thorax. The juncture of its thorax and abdomen even narrows a bit in a manner similar to the hornet that may be the model for natural selection of these traits. Like the bee flies, the Syrphid flies do not sting.

Fake Bumblebees

Also members of the Syrphidae family, species in the genus *Mallota* are often mistaken for bumblebees. One species, known by its scientific name of *Mallota posticata*, is about an inch (2.5 cm) long and has the same yellow and black, furry body of its counterpart. The only giveaway, again, is the pair of mammoth fly eyes. Other species, such as *Mallota bautias*, are smaller, but are still dead ringers for bumblebees.

Moth Flies

Although any advantage gained from their mimicry remains unclear, certain species of flies in the family Psychodidae resemble small moths. Small in size at less than a half inch (1.3 cm), the typical moth fly has a large, fur-covered thorax, elongated antennae, and grand, often patterned wings. People occasionally see them around a shower drain, where they eat fungus and algae that thrive in damp areas.

SPECIFICATIONS

Insects: Flies, gnats, mosquitoes, midges, no-see-ums (punkies), and others.
Order: Diptera
Meaning of Diptera: "two wings," referring to the single pair of large flight wings
Typical characteristics of adults in this order:
• one pair of noticeable, transparent flight wings, although some are wingless
• one pair of halteres, which are tiny, knoblike structures behind the much larger forewings
• mouthparts modified for sucking, sponging, or lapping up fluids, and sometimes also for piercing
• females of many species drink blood (for egg production)
• larvae that are called maggots in many species, and wigglers, grubs, or simply larvae in others
DIVERSITY
Number of known species: 120,000 to 150,000
Size: Many of the smaller members of the order, such as the gnats and midges, may be only 0.08 inches (2 mm) long. The largest is a South American species, *Gauromydas heros*, which has a body length of 2.4 inches (6 cm).
Sampling of benefits to humans: Many flies are pollinators of plants, including crops. Some species in this order are also predators of pest insects, such as aphids.

When looking at this close-up of the drab flesh fly of the family Calliphoridae, it is hard to believe that related species are such successful mimics of more exotic insect species.

Those big fly eyes may be giveaways, but from even a slight distance this female syrphid fly is a dead ringer for a fuzzy bumblebee.

Beetle and Moth Mimics

Another wasp mimic, the locust borer beetle (*Megacyllene robinae*) is considered a pest insect. It lays its eggs in locust trees, where the larvae bore into the wood and weaken the branches.

A fly that looks like a bee is easier to fathom than a moth or a beetle donning the same disguise. Still, they do exist. Like the bee flies, the moths and beetles gain some protection by resembling a dangerous species. This kind of simulation is called Batesian mimicry, and also includes instances in which an insect appears similar to a noxious species. Batesian mimicry is named after Henry Walter Bates, a nineteenth-century British naturalist who spent more that 10 years scouring South America and the Amazon for interesting insect species.

Clearwing Moths

The notion that a moth can pass for a wasp seems far-fetched, until one of the wasp-resembling clearwing moths alights nearby. The furry bodies of these insects, members of the family Sessiidae, are striped in yellow and black and have a set of long, narrow wings much more closely resemble those of a wasp than the wider wings usually associated with moths. A number of these moths, including the lilac borers and ash borers (both in the species *Podosesia syringae*), even hold their wings straight back as a wasp does. The lilac and ash borers are both considered pests because their caterpillars feed inside the stems of shrubs or trees, where they can cause considerable damage.

Beetles

Many of the bee-copying beetles have a dark-and-light color pattern on their abdomens as well as their elytra, the hard forewings that lie atop and conceal the abdomen when the beetle is at rest. An example of a bee imitator is the hairy flower scarab (*Trichiotinus rufobrunneus*). Along with its brown–and-yellow markings, this species has the fuzzy body and head typical of many bees.

Some longhorn beetles in the family Cerambycidae bear a strong resemblance to wasps. Like the hairy flower scarab, some longhorn beetles have patterned elytra that cover the entire abdomen. The tiger longicorn (*Aridaeus thoracicus*) is a species with black stripes on a mainly orange body. A few species, such as *Hesthesis variegata*, have unusually short elytra that do not cover the black-and-orange abdomen or the long dark-brown hind wings. In most beetles, the elytra lie out of the way, so that the filmy hind wings beneath them can unfold for flight. In this species, however, the orange-and-black elytra remain atop the thorax, thus maintaining their ruse, and the hind wings are still able to unfurl for flight. They can therefore keep up the complete wasp masquer-ade whether they are on the ground or in the air.

TOTALLY WASTED

The Florida tortoise beetle (*Hemisphaerota cyanea*) is truly one of the world's greatest recyclers.

When an adult female, which is round, purple, and about three-sixteenths of an inch (0.5 cm) long, lays her eggs, she covers them up with a blanket made of her own waste pellets. The reuse of excrement extends to her newborns. Each larva releases long strands of feces and fashions them into a thatchlike home for itself. With its fecal protection in place, the larva remains there, pupates, and eventually emerges as an adult beetle. The shield is not a foolproof one. Although it does deter some of its would-be predators, it is no match for a carabid beetle known by the scientific name of *Calleida viridipennis*. This beetle either munches through the fecal strands or nudges its way through them to reach the underlying larva, which it then devours.

Above: Three hairy flower scarab beetles (*Trichiotinus rufobrunneus*) appear to nestle inside the flowers they feed on. North American natives, these beetles are often found feeding on the nectar, pollen, and petals of various flowers, in open areas near woodland.

Left: What looks like a clump of hay or thatch is really the larva of a tortoise beetle. The thatchlike covering is actually feces.

CHAPTER 6

ACTIVE DEFENSE

BESIDES BLENDING INTO THE BACKGROUND or copying the appearance of another predator-unfriendly species, insects have various other adaptations for defending themselves against their enemies. Occasionally, it is the attacker, rather than the prey, that winds up on the wrong end of the stick. Seemingly vulnerable caterpillars are particularly adept at turning the tables on a would-be attacker by inflicting it with a stinging jolt. Other insects with strong defensive tactics are those that repel predators by tossing up their stomach contents, by oozing blood, or by producing a hot, noxious, and sometimes blinding spray.

For certain insects, their answer lies in a bluff. From adult moths and butterflies to caterpillars, grasshoppers, and beetles, numerous insects flash usually hidden markings or bright hues when a predator nears. In some cases, the predator may think it is faced with an insect much larger than it expected or with one of its own attackers. Even if the predator does not itself immediately flee, the prey insect frequently gains at least a split-second escape window and puts it to good use. An insect without any of these attributes is still usually a master of evasion. Those skills are evident to anyone who has ever tried to catch a cockroach or nab a whirligig beetle barehanded.

Left: As its name implies, the owl butterfly (*Calligo eurilochus*) displays a pair of owl-like eyes on its wings. The trick is to make a predator think it's facing an even larger predator. Inset: The owl butterfly may rely on a sight-based warning, but the green stinkbug goes straight for the nose: a foul-smelling, nasty-tasting secretion keeps most enemies at bay.

Spines and Stinging

With their soft bodies and slow movements, caterpillars should be the poster children for easy-to-eat meals. They do, however, have a few tricks up their sleeves, or more accurately, along their bodies.

The bright circus hues of the saddleback caterpillar (*Acharia stimulea*) may invite a closer look, but beware the fuzzy projections—they are actually poisonous spines.

The Saddleback Caterpillar

The inch-long (2.5 cm) saddleback caterpillar (*Acharia stimulea*) is not as gentle as its clownish dress would imply. It is brown with a kelly green, white-outlined, saddle-shaped mark on its back. Tall, hair-covered projections, or tubercles, rise from the head and tail ends. Its appearance nearly begs children to pick it up, but this is a mistake. The innocuous-looking hairs are actually venomous spines that

break off on contact, often producing a burning pain akin to a bee sting. A species of eastern North America, it eventually becomes a comparatively bland gray-and-brown moth with a 1- to 1.7-inch (2.5–4.3 cm) wingspan.

Buck Moth Caterpillar

Hairier than the saddleback, this caterpillar (*Hemileuca maia*) is also equipped with venom delivered by its bristly stinging spines. The caterpillar, which can reach 2 to 2.5 inches (5.1–6.4 cm) long, may be brown, purplish, or black with white mottling along its sides, a brick-red head, and numerous short spiny tufts arranged periodically along its back. This eastern North American species transforms into a moth sporting white-banded brown wings and a hoar-frosted gray body with a noticeably rust-tinted rear end.

Stinging Rose Caterpillar

A lovely larva, this caterpillar (*Parasa indetermina*) could have been painted by an artist. A set of four, fine, black pinstripes runs down the center of its back, and a bold combination of red bars and spots usually decorates each side. In addition, pairs of large, yellow, spine-covered tubercles arise from the back, and numerous smaller groupings of hairs poke above the surface in between. The spines of the stinging

the spine breaks off, the venom oozes into the victim, usually causing initial pain along with a bump.

BLISTER BEETLE BLOOD

The blood—technically called the hemolymph—of the blister beetles causes the human skin reaction that gives these insects their name. People usually encounter blister beetles when standing near an outdoor light at night. The beetles, which are attracted to the illumination, sometimes pause on a person's body. Even a light brush that does no real damage to them provokes bleeding. This is known as reflex bleeding and occurs in a number of insects. What is different about the blister beetle is the chemical in its blood. Called cantharidin, it is about as toxic as cyanide if ingested and can raise blisters if touched. Although unsightly, the blisters are generally short-lived and have no lasting effects.

Above left: If disturbed or brushed against, the blister beetle of the family Meloidae will shed its own blood—which contains a chemical as toxic as cyanide and strong enough to blister human skin.

Below: The vividly colored stinging rose slug caterpillar virtually carries a warning sign to stay away; unwary predators will get a dose of venom from its numerous spines or tubercles.

rose caterpillar, also known as a rose slug caterpillar, discharge their venom to predators that overlook the larva's warning coloration and venture to take a nip out of it. Also a resident of eastern North America, it develops into a brown moth with wide green markings on its forewings and thorax.

Billygoat Plum Caterpillar

Australia's billygoat plum caterpillar (*Thosea penthima*) likewise has numerous spines along its body. It is lemon-colored with a double row of blue spots down the middle of its back and additional blue spots along each side. As an adult moth, it is almost uniformly brown, except for a thin, dark stripe on each forewing. Like other stinging caterpillars, it is endowed with hollow spines, each with a poison gland at its base. When the

Compelling Repellents

The insects in the following group lack stingers, but they possess weapons nonetheless. Each is capable of warding off many an attacker by spraying, oozing, or regurgitating noxious substances.

Whirligigs

Whirligigs (*Dineutes hornii*) are the small, round, black beetles that zip along in convoluted, frequently circular paths across the surface of still water. Found nearly worldwide, whirligigs have an effective security system. When their bodies receive a squeeze, they release a white substance from glands near the rump. This substance, which smells a bit like apples, protects them from one of their mortal enemies, a fish that many anglers know well: the largemouth bass (*Micropterus salmoides*). According to Cornell University research reported in 2000, a bass will suck a beetle into its mouth, then take in added water, spit out the insect, and repeat the process a few more times. The researchers surmised that the bass was attempting to rinse off the offending goop from what would otherwise be a nice little treat. Experiments showed that an average hungry but not famished fish would rinse the beetle for 78 seconds before giving up and moving on to another

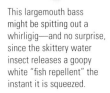

This largemouth bass might be spitting out a whirligig—and no surprise, since the skittery water insect releases a goopy white "fish repellent" the instant it is squeezed.

prey. Here, a beetle's patience pays off; it is typically able to ration out the white secretion for 90 seconds, giving it just enough of an edge to survive the confrontation.

A Sickening Method

Children sometimes call it tobacco juice, but the thin, brown syrup oozing out from between a captured grasshopper's jaws is actually its stomach contents. Although it may not be the most elegant defensive tactic, throwing up is an effective deterrent, especially if the grasshopper has recently eaten certain plants. In fact, scientists have found that it is the semidigested plants and not the additional components, such as saliva and other digestive juices, that turn off attackers. Fortunately for the grasshopper, predators decide quickly—often before swallowing— that a grasshopper has a nasty taste and spit it out alive and in one piece.

Ready, Aim, Fire

A number of insects do more than ooze foul fluids: they shoot them. One example is the two-striped stick insect (*Anisomorpha bupestroides*). Although it appears harmless enough with its slow movements and its long, thin body and legs, the stick insect not only secretes a chemical substance when it feels threatened, but it can also spray it more than a foot (30.5 cm) away. On the rare occasion when the fluid hits the eyes of a predator, it can cause temporary blindness.

Another spraying insect is the bombardier beetle (*Stenaptinus insignis*), a considerable marksman with a boiling-hot defensive spray. This black-and-orange beetle from Africa can aim in any direction from a nozzle in its rear end, and it can fire at least 20 times in a row before running out of ammunition. To top it off, each shot is accompanied by a popping sound. As might be expected, the combination effectively protects it from its predators.

NOW THAT STINKS

The stinkbug really does stink. This bug, which has a body shaped like the shield on a highway sign, secretes a vile-smelling and nasty-tasting fluid from the sides of its body. Although one might think that other animals would turn up their noses at any of the various species of stinkbugs (all in the family Pentatomidae), birds, spiders, and other predators regularly eat many of them. A few stinkbugs, however, prove just too disgusting for a predator to palate. One is the harlequin stinkbug (*Murgantia histrionica*). This striking yellow-and-black bug parades around during the daylight hours as if flaunting its offensive characteristics, daring a predator to take a bite.

The beetle is able to produce the spray without boiling its own body because the spray becomes hot only at the moment it is made. Up until then, the two chemicals that combine to make the spray remain in separate compartments in the insect's body. Researchers still wonder, however, how the beetles withstand the heat and irritation once they start spraying, since they usually become soaked with it during their battles.

Repellents are not foolproof—some hungry birds and spiders will actually overlook both the bad smell and terrible taste of the stinkbug.

With the aim of a marksman, the bombardier beetle can shoot a boiling-hot, noxious fluid from its rear end up to 20 times in row—all accompanied by popping sound effects.

Startling Bluff

Small children love to scare their older brothers and sisters or a parent by jumping from behind a couch or door, usually with hands held high into "claws" and accompanied by a loud growl. The same thing happens in the insect world, but here, the ploy's degree of success can be the difference between life and death.

My, What Big Eyes You Have!

A bird spies a polyphemus moth (*Anthera polyphemus*) sitting on a tree trunk and swoops down for the kill. In the moment before the bird strikes, however, two huge owl eyes appear out of nowhere. The bird makes an emergency swerve and aborts the attack. But the "owl eyes" that scared it off were really just wing markings. As the moth spreads its front wings wide, it reveals its hind pair, each of which is embellished with a large, oval, blue-and-yellow eyespot. These very prominent eyespots inspired its common name, polyphemus—the same as the one-eyed giant of Greek mythology. Eyespots are common on moths, where they remain out of sight on the hind wings until the insect flashes them. Numerous butter-flies have eyespots, too, but they are often on the top surface of both the

Above: There's double trouble when the poly-phemus moth (*Anthera polyphemus*) shifts its wings to reveal two sets of birdlike eyespots guaranteed to confuse approaching predators.

Right: Known as yellow-and-black poison-arrow frogs or bumblebee poison frogs for their colorful backs, the highly toxic poison dart frogs (*Dendrobates leucomelas*) of Central America are the top of a poison "food chain" that starts with organic toxins consumed by ants, which the frogs then ingest.

front and hind wings. Because a butter-fly often perches with its wings together over its back and only the bottom sides showing, it can simply open the wings to expose the eyespots. In both but-terflies and moths, scientists believe

TOXIC DIETS

If some insects accumulate toxins from the plants they eat, what happens to the vertebrate animals that dine on the insects? In animals such as the poison dart frogs of Central America and the pitohui birds of New Guinea, they become toxic, too. Scientists now believe that the pitohui, a bright orange-and-black bird, gets its toxin from one part of its diet, small beetles in the genus *Choresine*. The frogs get their preda-tor-dissuading poison from ants that are members of the large subfamily known as Formicinae. These ants contain pumiliotoxin, an alkaloid toxin. Researchers speculate that the ants may, in turn, obtain the poison from items in their own diet. Interestingly, the colorful poison dart frogs on display in most zoos and aquariums are usually not poisonous at all, because their diet in the artificial habitat typically contains none of the poison-conferring ants.

the eyespots serve the same purpose: to scare off or at least momentarily startle predators so that the prey insect has time to make its escape.

Snake Eyes

If a caterpillar lacks camouflage, stinging hairs, or a bad taste, how can it avoid predators? For several swallowtails, the answer is to look like something threatening . . . say, a snake. The caterpillar of the spicebush swallowtail (*Papilio troilus*) of North America does just that. When this yellowish-green, sometimes jade larva feels threatened, it rears up its body, displays a black marking that could double for a snake's open gape, and compounds the hoax by swelling up its thorax to showcase two prominent black-and-orange eyespots. The result is the semblance of a small viper. Another example of a bluffing caterpillar is Australia's wattle moth (*Neola semiaurata*). This larva has two heads—one real and the other a fake that is located at the opposite end of the caterpillar. Its defense is to lift its abdomen, which is adorned with hornlike projections. The movement reveals a pair of otherwise-concealed, dark eyespots. As might be expected, the bluffs of both caterpillars, as well as other similarly endowed species, are enough to discourage many a predator.

This nominally defenseless spicebush swallowtail larva has puffed up the markings on its thorax to create two "eyes" that lend it the menacing appearance of a snake.

Flashy Dodge

Some insects rely on a surprise burst of color or an unexpected noise (and sometimes both) to startle a predator and give themselves a split second to exit the area. Beetles and grasshoppers employ these tactics. The click beetles in the family Elateridae use noise and movement to escape a predator. When alarmed, they can flex their bodies and snap into the air, giving the attacker quite a surprise. Some grasshoppers, especially the band-winged grasshoppers in the subfamily Oedipodinae, make a faint ticking sound as they flip out their brightly hued hind wings and leap into flight. The combination of noise and color flash provides a momentary diversion and may be enough to secure the insect's getaway.

Fleeing Insects

Insects with defense tactics that fall short for whatever reason can always try to escape by whatever means of locomotion they have. Whether it is running, jumping, flying, or swimming, the purpose is the same—to get away as quickly as possible.

Sprinting Cockroaches

Cockroaches are typically nocturnal creatures that hide out during the day, usually in a dark and damp or humid spot. Occasionally people catch a fleeting glimpse of one of them in a house, typically after switching on the kitchen or bathroom light late at night. It is then that the cockroach's power of retreat shines. At about 5 feet (1.5 meters) per second, cockroaches are fast, and they attain that speed almost instantaneously, making a beeline for cover before the human spotter has a chance to do anything. Occasionally an especially alert person is able to deliver a stomp with a shoe or a blow with a rolled-up magazine before the cockroach reaches a protected spot, but even a direct hit may not spell doom for the insect. Because of its flat body and black, armorlike exoskeleton, it can almost miraculously survive such encounters unscathed and when the shoe lifts continues running as if nothing had happened. With such speed and resilience, cockroaches rarely resort to using their wings for locomotion, although most are competent fliers.

Leapers and Springers

"Any place is better than here" could be the motto of the jumping insects, most of which have little if any control over where they land or even whether they land right-side up. The tiny snowfleas, which look like little more than black specks on the snow, and the click beetles, which can be an inch (2.5 cm) long or more, are both springers that may travel through the air while doing barrel rolls, landing only a short distance away. Grasshoppers are other noted jumpers. Although they are adequate fliers, they sometimes simply leap, frequently landing with an awkward somersault or with a sideways slide across the pavement, and are occasionally stopped short by the side of a garage or other obstruction.

Above: An evolutionary masterpiece, the cockroach uses lightning speed to avoid a death blow, and its flat, plated body makes it hard to kill, even after being stepped on.

Right: Although the large eyespots of this eyed click beetle from North Carolina are one type of defense, this insect is best known for flipping into the air and somersaulting to escape its enemies.

Skimmers and Divers

The whirligigs, already mentioned earlier for the repellant that they ooze, are also excellent at evading predators with their breakneck speed and the fancy moves they make while scooting across the surface of the water. Children and adults alike can spend hours chasing them and have few insects to show for the effort. Another skill that makes them especially difficult to catch is their diving ability. They usually only resort to this escape maneuver when capture is imminent. As a predator comes close, the beetle dips below the water's surface and out of reach, only to reappear a few moments later in another spot.

The Aerialists

Of all of the flying insects, perhaps none are more accomplished at avoiding predators than the dragonflies. Along with their enormous, motion-detecting eyes and great speed, they have astounding maneuverability. They can turn on a dime, almost literally. In just one body length, a dragonfly can angle right or left, up or down, and even spin 180 degrees, and then head off in the new direction. Like hummingbirds, dragonflies are also able to hover in place and fly backward to not only avoid predators, but also to find prey. They are masters at snatching flying insects right out of the air.

Fruit flies (family Drosophilidae) appear to be spectacularly evasive fliers, too. Much of their prowess at circumventing annihilation from the swat of a human hand, however, has to do with physics rather than their aerial skills. Because they are so small and light, the rush of air caused by the swat itself actually pushes the fruit fly out of the way. The human is left with an empty hand and generally an unpleasant word on the lips.

Background above: Top honors for aerial maneuvering must go to the dragonfly, which can spin 180 degrees in midflight and zoom off in the opposite direction.

Left: When threatened or sensing danger, a fire ant can "sound" an alarm by releasing a pheromone that brings its colony mates scurrying for battle.

DANGER! DANGER!

When an ant finds a food source, it lays down a trail of chemicals, called pheromones, for its nest mates to follow. This is not their only pheromone, however. Ants typically have another that signals not food but instead danger. An example of this chemical can be seen among the South American fire ant (*Solenopsis saevissima*), red-bodied insects that grow to about 0.4 inches (0.9 cm) long. When a fire ant perceives a threat, it releases its alarm pheromone, quickly triggering other ants to rush in and prepare for battle. Other species of ants have similar pheromones that call in the troops.

CHAPTER 7

ON THE ATTACK

FEW THINGS CAN ENERGIZE A RELAXING PICNIC like the arrival of bees and wasps. Gyrations, yelps, and arm-waving are common picnicker reactions, even though most of us have been stung only rarely and even then, experienced just mild, short-lived pain. These flying insects have gained our respect, however, earned or not. Another frequent picnic-crasher and noted member of the stinging-insect category is the ant. Although a minority of these three insect groups have stingers that inflict much damage to the average human, many bees, wasps, and ants present a formidable defense and daunting offense that places them high on the list of most-dangerous insects.

Other nonstinging insects are no less perilous to their prey. A praying mantid, for example, can strike out so quickly with its strong, raptorial forelegs that a flying insect frequently cannot become airborne in time to avoid its clutches. Speed is not the only weapon that a nonstinging insect may rely on. Several relatively slow-moving insects, such as the caddisfly and the antlion, use traps of varying kinds to gain their next meals.

Left: Proof that there is power in numbers, these honey bees create an impressive display as they swarm around their queen on an Australian eucalyptus branch. Inset: Ants might seem small and insignificant, yet they are organized and resourceful—and those powerful jaws can inflict a painful bite, even to humans.

Bee and Wasp Venom

Not all bee and wasp species possess stingers, and among those that do, they are limited to the females because the stinger is really a modified egg-laying structure. Much of the stinger's punch comes from the small venom sac at its base. As the stinger plunges into the skin, it delivers the venom from the sac as a hypodermic needle would inject medicine. Most bees and wasps pull out the stingers intact, and use them again and again over a lifetime. The honey bee is different, however; its stinger is barbed and cannot be retracted. Instead, the stinger, along with the venom sac and some of its surrounding musculature, tears free of the bee and stays in the skin, where it continues to pump venom into the victim. The bee loses a good part of its abdomen in the process, and it dies shortly thereafter.

These wasps, seen clustering around a hummingbird feeder, are one of the stinging insects that inspire great caution in humans—not only is their sting painful, but they also often attack in groups.

Gang Violence

Bees and wasps inspire such respect partly because certain species live in groups, and sometimes launch joint attacks. Single stings typically are only life-threatening to victims who are allergic to bee venom, but many dozens of simultaneous stings can be hazardous to anyone. According to the Agricultural Research Service of the U.S. Department of Agriculture: "The average person can safely tolerate 10 stings per pound of body weight. This means that although 500 stings could kill a child, the average adult could withstand more than 1,100 stings." Elderly adults and young children, however, may be especially susceptible to the stings, and may succumb to far fewer of them. Fortunately, most bees and wasps are either solitary insects or live in small nests with a few members, and exhibit nonaggressive tendencies.

Killer Bees

Unlike most other bees and wasps, the so-called killer bees are combative. The bees themselves are all descendants of a group of queen honey bees that geneticist Warwick Kerr imported to southern Brazil from Africa in 1956. He crossbred other races, or subspecies, of honey bees in the species *Apis mellifera* to generate more-productive honey makers that were better adapted to survival in the region. In some of his experiments, in which he mated the African bees with other races already living in the New World, he found that the hives were especially quick to respond to perceived threats by mounting concerted attacks. In the following year, the bees in more than two dozen of these unusually aggressive hives escaped to the wild. Since then, they have bred successfully with other bees and migrated farther and farther from Brazil, especially to the west and the north, at about 200 to 375 miles (330–600 km) a year. They first reached the United States in 1990. As of 2005, they had spread to many southern states and were continuing to move northward.

These Africanized bees earned the name "killer bees" for good reason. Although their sting is no more potent than that of the average honey bee, killer bees attack in numbers with far less provocation than their counterparts. For example, a lawn mower or other vibrating motor running too near a killer-bee nest is enough to incite a massive response, and the bees

will not only attack but also pursue the target for as far as a quarter of a mile (0.4 km). Numerous encounters have resulted in human deaths, including the first U.S. fatality in Texas in 1993 when a 82-year-old man was repeatedly stung as he attempted to ignite a nest to remove it from a house.

Left: An unwelcome import to Brazil, African bees soon interbred with local honey bees, forming an aggressive hybrid. These Africanized "killer" bees, seen forming a comb in a tree, will attack in great numbers with only slight provocation.

Below: Though there are many folk remedies for a bee sting, from baking soda and mud to a slice of onion or a dollop of tobacco juice, people with serious allergies to stings need to carry an epinephrine kit when spending time outdoors.

NOW THAT HURTS

For the average person, the sting from a bee smarts and sometimes burns for a few moments, and perhaps rises into a small bump that may last for a couple of hours. Although folk remedies can range from a slice of onion to a gob of tobacco juice, modern medical professionals typically recommend straightforward home care, with steps such as removing any stinger left in the skin, washing the wound site, and applying ice to treat the welt. Some people, however, are allergic to bee venom and need immediate medical attention. Their symptoms may include a dramatic drop in blood pressure, swelling of the face, and difficulty breathing, among others. People who know they are allergic to bee stings often carry with them an epinephrine kit so that they can temporarily minister to themselves before heading to the doctor.

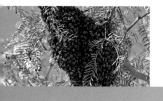

Beware the Ant

Ants are tougher than they look. They typically have large, powerful jaws for their size and a pheromone-mediated "mob mentality" that makes good use of their large numbers. Some have the added weapon of venomous stings that can immobilize or kill much larger insects and sometimes other organisms. In addition, many use unusual methods of ambushing their prey and their in-family rivals.

Fire Ants

Fire ants are small ants, but they pack a wallop, as anyone who has accidentally bumped into one of their mounded nests can verify. The typically red, or red-and-black ants swarm out, often by the hundreds, and begin inflicting painful, venomous stings, which kill tissue in the immediate area and result in pus-filled bumps that may last for a few days. For people who are allergic to the venom, the experience can be deadly.

Several species of fire ants exist (all in the genus *Solenopsis*). The first species came to the United States accidentally from South America in 1918, and others followed. The ants have now spread to at least 11 states from Texas to Florida, and up to North Carolina and Tennessee, and researchers are scrambling to find ways to control them. One eradication option includes the introduction of a fly with an intriguing and completely accurate common name. The decapitating fly (*Pseudacteon tricuspis*) lays its eggs on the body of the imported red fire ant (*Solenopsis invicta*). The egg hatches into a larva, which proceeds to move into the ant's head and feed on the tissues it finds there. When the larva is ready to pupate, the ant's head falls off. If it drops while the ant is in the nest, the other ants carry the severed head outside for disposal. There, the fly emerges from its pupa, soon ready to find the next fire ant for its own generation.

Sneak Attack

A young katydid walks along a branch of a tree in French Guiana north of Brazil. As it steps onto a mat of fungus, it feels something in the mat grabbing at its legs and antennae. As it soon becomes trapped, ants rush to the young katydid, stinging it until it stops moving. Although the victim was unaware of it, the fungus mat was a trap constructed by the ants, according to researchers at Toulouse and Blaise Pascal universities in France, and the University of

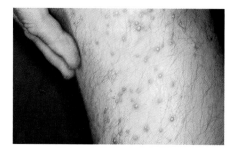

Watch your step! This unwary scientist was stung more than 250 times in less than 10 seconds when he carelessly knelt on a collapsed fire ant mound.

Illinois at Urbana-Champaign. The ants (*Allomerus decemarticulatus*) make the traps by snipping tiny hairs off a tree stem and fashioning them into a flat scaffold onto which fungus grows. The ants then lie in wait below for an insect to hazard past. From their position, the ants reach through spaces in the fungus mat to grasp passersby with their jaws and hold them until other ants can arrive to subdue the prey. According to the researchers, their discovery marks the first time ants have been shown to work together on building and using a trap.

Queen-ordered Infighting

Like a TV show mob boss who orders a hit on a rival, the top ant—the queen—in a Brazilian colony instructs her female underlings to attack those members of the nest that she regards as threats to her position. According to researchers at the Pierre and Marie Curie University in Paris and the universities of Sheffield and Keele in the United Kingdom, this rare kind of ordered "hit" occurs in *Dinoponera quadriceps*, a species of gigantic ants that grow to 1.2 inches (3 cm) in body length. Among this species, any of the females in the nest can battle their way to the top spot and become the queen. This is not as easy as it might seem. When the queen becomes aware of a rival, she slathers it with a chemical

THREE-LANE ANT HIGHWAYS

If we drove like some ants travel, our roads would have three lanes instead of two. We would take the two outer lanes to work and the inner one back home. Researchers Iain Couzin of Princeton University and Nigel Franks of the University of England used mathematical computer models and direct observations to figure out how the thousands-strong marches of South American army ants (*Eciton burchelli*) remain organized enough to keep flowing, especially when half of the ants are moving in the opposite direction from the others. They discovered that those heading to a food source give way to those carrying prey back to the nest, therefore splitting the outgoing traffic into two lanes with the incoming ants marching up the middle. The feat is especially remarkable considering the size of the marching hordes: up to 200,000 ants.

she releases from her abdomen. The chemical serves as a call to arms, and the other ants in the colony rush in to pin down the foe, sometimes for days on end. They finally release the defeated ant, which rejoins the nest but attempts no further coups. The queen's mob rule only lasts so long, however, and eventually one of the other six or seven dozen ants in the nest deposes her and takes over.

Above: No traffic jams here: like their South American kin, as African army ants (*Dorylus* species) go on the march, they leave a central lane free for ants carrying food and supplies back to the nest.

Background left: An insect familiar to most everyone, a common black ant investigates a flower.

Pit Traps

is older, it will metamorphose into a large-winged, slender-bodied adult that flits about in a rather lazy fashion. Until then, it remains underground, prepared to pierce its jaws into the next ant or other small insect that slides into its pit. Once it has a firm grip, it slowly pulls the victim deeper and deeper underground. There, it injects the prey with its saliva, waits for the saliva to begin liquefying the prey's innards, and then sucks out the soupy bodily fluids. The antlion eventually flings the leftover shell of the body out of the trap and settles in for the next kill.

Pit Construction

The antlion builds its trap itself. It first finds a suitable spot by wandering

Above: Usually found lurking at the bottom of a sandy pit or a wooden declivity, the antlion larva waits for passing insects to fall in and then uses its spectacular jaws to restrain the unlucky prey.

In sandy soil, sometimes under the eave of a building or below a deck, a predator lurks in the innocuous looking, cone-shaped depressions that disrupt the surface. These pits, usually 1 to 2 inches (2.5–5.1 cm) across and an inch (2.5 cm) deep, are death traps to ants and other small, walking insects, because at the base of each pit are the needle-sharp tips of a pair of long jaws.

Antlions

The jaws belong to an antlion larva, one of several species in the family Myrmeleontidae and the order Neuroptera. When the antlion larva

TYING ONE ON

Carnivorous caterpillars are rare, and one that eats snails is rarer still. The larva of a small Hawaiian moth is one of the meat-eaters. It lives inside a hollow, tube-shaped, silken case that it creates, which it drags around as it slowly hunts for snails. What makes the caterpillar extraordinarily curious is its habit of using its silk to tie down a snail before venturing into the shell to dine on the meal inside. According to the University of Hawaii scientists who studied it, the caterpillar is the first mollusk-eating caterpillar ever described. Its new species name reflects its unusual lifestyle: *Hyposmocoma molluscivora*.

just below the surface of the ground, leaving visible trails in its wake. The trails, which resemble the doodles some people draw while talking on the phone or daydreaming, give the antlion larvae their other common name: doodlebugs. The larva decides on a location, usually under a deck, beneath the protection of building eave, or in some other a dry spot with loose and often sandy soil. There, it scoots backward into the soil and starts circling downward while flicking bits of soil up and out with its head. Soon, it has constructed a circular pit that narrows from the top down, and it buries itself at the bottom of the cone to begin its vigil.

How It Works

Loose, dry soil is key to the trap's success. The trap's only requirement is for an ant or another small insect to walk along the surface, step over the trap's edge, and begin its downward slide. Even if the prey insect happens to avoid the skewering antlion jaws at the bottom, its fate may be sealed. The soil grains continue to slide with each frenzied step it takes up the sides, sending it time and again to the waiting jaws. The antlion makes matters worse by flipping sand at the prey as it tries to climb, often hastening its fall back down.

These typical antlion pits excavated from loose, sandy soil are created by an antlion circling downward and flicking particles of dirt up and out with its head.

MEAT-EATING BEES

Not all bees are flower children. Some species tear bits of flesh from the bodies of dead animals, and at least one species will move in on a recently deserted wasp nest to get at the now-defenseless wasp eggs, larvae, and pupae left behind, say researchers from the University of São Paulo in Brazil. The South American bees known by the scientific name of *Trigona hypogea* chew up the still-living feast and then fly back to their own nest, where they mix the regurgitated wasp meat with a sugary substance that acts as a preservative. This species is the fourth bee shown to eat meat, whether living or dead. To the relief of nightmare-prone children everywhere, no bees are known to have a taste for live human flesh.

Gone Fishing

Although it may seem more in keeping with the behavior of a cartoon insect rather than a real one, some species are able to spin a some-times-elaborate fishing net and use it to catch their prey. They are the larvae of caddisflies.

Case-building Caddisflies

Adult caddisflies are land-living insects that fly about at night and rest in out-of-the-way locations by day. They have large wings, a characteristic that frequently leads people to misidentify them as moths. During the few weeks caddisflies live as adults, they get to the business of mating and laying eggs. The females—wings and all—enter the water to lay their eggs on the sides of submerged rocks or other hard surfaces. In some species, the eggs hatch into

The caddisfly larva lives underwater and carries its home on its back while scouring the streambed for algae and tiny inverte-brates. The larva constructs it bejeweled-like case out of pebbles and strands of silk produced from glands in its mouth.

larvae, each of which almost imme-diately begins building a tube-shaped case that will serve as its aquatic home. The larva constructs the case with a combination of silk that it produces from glands near its mouth and small objects, such as fragments of vegetation, from its surroundings. The case often resembles a small piece of mushy stick.

These case-building caddisflies do their feeding without using nets. Instead, each simply pokes its head and front legs out of the end of the case and crawls along the stream bottom, drag-ging its case with it and consuming bits of algae, tiny invertebrates, and other scraps of food it may find. As the larva grows, it continually adds more mate-rial to its case to match its size. When it has grown to its full size, it attaches its case to a rock, shell, plant, or other substrate, and after a short period, usu-ally two weeks in typical case-building caddisflies in the genus *Limnephilus*, the pupa emerges from the case, makes its way to the surface, and there transforms into its winged adult form.

Net-making Caddisflies

Species in three families of caddisflies—Philopotamidae, Polycentropodidae, and Hydropsychidae—use their silk to build nets that they use for filtering food from the water. Depending on the species, the net may have a variety of

"If all mankind were to disappear, the world would regenerate back to the rich state of equilibrium that existed ten thousand years ago. If insects were to vanish, the environment would collapse into chaos."

—EDWARD O. WILSON

SPECIFICATIONS

Insects: Caddisflies

Order: Trichoptera

Meaning of Trichoptera: "hair wing," referring to the delicate hairs, called setae, sprouting on the wings

Typical characteristics of adults in this order:

- wings covered with tiny, fine hairs
- chewing mouthparts
- usually hold the wings angled over their backs to form a peak
- many are mostly active at night
- in some species, the larvae build hollow tubes of sand, bits of leaves, and other material, and have nicknames such as caddisworms, casemakers, rock rollers, and stick bait

DIVERSITY

Number of known species: 7,000 to 10,000

Size: The microcaddisflies are among the smallest members of the order, and may reach only 0.04 to 0.08 inches (1–2 mm) in body length as adults. Caddisflies in the genus *Hydatophylax* are some of the largest adult members, and grow to about an inch (2.5 cm) long.

Sampling of benefits to humans:

Caddisflies are bioindicators of water quality: their presence indicates a clean and healthy stream. Anglers often model their lures, known as flies, on caddisflies. People also occasionally make jewelry from caddisfly cocoons.

and occasionally doing repair work on the mesh. The net also provides a measure of protection. When the larva senses a threat, it can retreat to a recess in the net and wait there for the danger to pass.

Bioindicators

Ecologists sometimes use the animals living in an area to inform them about the health of the ecosystem. Caddisfly larvae have long been known as reliable graders, or bioindicators, of stream quality. As a testament to the larvae's dependability, scientists frequently search for caddisfly larvae and certain other insects as primary sources of information on freshwater quality. If the insects are present in good numbers, the stream is likely to be clean. Another regularly used insect bioindicator for streams is the stonefly, an insect with a similarly long-winged, terrestrial adult as well as an aquatic larval stage with a strong preference for unpolluted waters. This insect, however, does not have a four-stage life cycle—egg to larva to pupa to adult—of the caddisfly. Instead, it has only three. The egg hatches into a larva, called an aquatic nymph or a naiad, that resembles a wingless adult. The naiad transforms into the adult. Stoneflies are also in a different order from the caddisflies: the order Plecoptera.

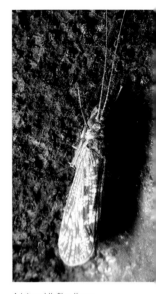

Adult caddisflies live a brief time—a few weeks at most—so must get busy procreating, which concludes with females returning to the water to lay their eggs.

forms, including a free-flowing funnel; a more stationary, half-dome or tent structure; or a haphazard-looking tangle that gives the appearance of a matted clump of wet spider webbing. Whatever the design, the silken nets are suited to their job of sifting tiny bits of plant matter and small invertebrates out of the water. The caddisfly larva moves along its net, picking out tasty morsels

PART 3

INSECT BEHAVIOR

CHAPTER 8

GETTING AROUND

ANY FORM OF LOCOMOTION any other animal uses, insects use too. Birds fly, and so do insects. Fish swim, and so do insects. Worms tunnel, frogs jump, and one lizard can even skip over the surface of the water. Ditto for the insects. When it comes to locomotion, insects are extremely versatile.

A person with the locomotive powers of a grasshopper, for instance, could take a leisurely stroll from home to school or work, or could instead decide to leap the route in minutes, or if the mood struck, could unfold a pair of flight wings and take to the air. A human endowed with a mosquito's abilities could fly for a while and take a break by clinging to a wall or walking across a ceiling. Likewise, a person who had the skills of some beetles could recover from an embarrassing situation by literally digging a hole and climbing into it . . . and then escape by tunneling away.

Insects' ability to get around in so many fashions has helped them invade nearly every tiny bit of land, spade full of dirt, and pool of freshwater anywhere on Earth. Of course, each individual insect cannot walk, fly, leap, swim, and tunnel, but whatever its method of locomotion, it is well suited to the way it lives.

Left: Some insects are amazing leapers. A typical grasshopper, for example, can jump distances equal to about 20 times its body length. Inset: Caterpillars are usually more interested in eating than in moving, but when necessary they use the curved hooks at the tips of their abdominal prolegs to climb. Pages 82–83: In a cross-species relationship that benefits both species, tiny aphids receive protection from much larger ants in exchange for the sweet liquid that they secrete.

In the Air

Of all of the flying animals living today—bats, birds, and insects—the insects have been flying the longest. In fact, insects were on the wing millions of years before birds and bats even appeared on Earth. Dragonflies, such as this male blue dasher (*Pachydiplax longipennis*), are some of the most adept of the insect fliers.

So-called flying squirrels, frogs, lizards, and even one species of snake do not actually fly. They can glide, but they lack wings for real flight. That leaves only three groups of animals that can truly fly: birds, bats, and insects.

Wing Design

Because insects have exoskeletons rather than internal bony skeletons like birds and bats, their wings are not the same as those of other fliers. Bird and bat wings are modified front legs, and their bones provide the underlying structure for the wings. Insect wings are completely different. These wings have nothing to do with the legs and

instead are outgrowths of the upper side of the thorax. In insects, this middle section of the body has three segments. Most adult insects have four wings, which arise from the last two of these segments. Rather than a wing of skin stretching between bones as in bats and birds, the wing of an insect is made of fingernail-like material, ranging from very thin to thick and tough, held in place by a scaffold of tubes, or veins. These carry air; insect "blood," called hemolymph; and nerves. The number and arrangement of the veins, which are often clearly visible, can be excellent clues for identifying the general type of adult insect and sometimes the exact species.

Taking Flight

Flight in an insect is an unusual process, especially when considering that the wings themselves have no muscles in them. All of the flight muscles are in the thorax, so the only part of the wing near the muscle is the end attaching to the thorax. Some insects, such as dragonflies and cockroaches, use the force of their muscles to pull or push directly on the base of the wings to make them flap. Dragonflies have separate muscles capable of moving each wing independently, making them extraordinarily maneuverable fliers. In other insects, however, the flight mechanism is an indirect one. Their muscles tug on the top and bottom of the thorax from the inside, changing its shape to make it flatter. This raises the wing. When the muscles relax, the thorax springs back to its original shape, flipping the wings back down. If the spring-back reverberates, the wing may flap additional times without any extra work on the part of the muscle. So few insects directly haul their wings up and down.

One Pair or Two?

Four wings flapping at the same time is not always a good thing. The front pair can disturb the air enough to disrupt the flight of the rear pair, and make for inefficient movement. Beetles and many other insects have solved the problem by lifting their front pair of wings out of the way of their hind wings, and letting the latter pair do most of the flying. Flies took another path. They use their forewings for flight, while little knobby structures, called halteres, have taken the place of their hind wings. The halteres are important for maintaining balance in flight.

Bees are some of the four-wing insect fliers. They keep their front and hind wings in sync with small hooks, essentially creating a single flight surface. Dragonflies, on the other hand, beat their four wings out of phase—one down on each side while the other is up—so they do not interfere with one another.

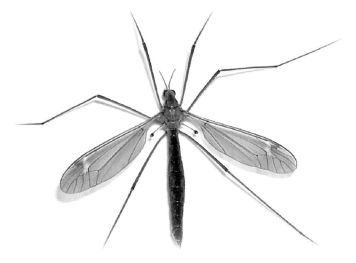

Above: As a group, flies are unusual because they have two large flight wings and two much smaller structures, called halteres, that take the place of hind wings. In some species, such as this crane fly, the knobby halteres are large enough to be easily seen.

Below: Halteres contain sensors to keep a fly on track, even in total darkness.

NIGHT FLIGHT

Just as a pilot can navigate his or her airplane at night or during a storm using only the instrument panel, a fly can stay airborne in pitch-dark conditions with its "instruments": the two halteres located where the hind flight wings would otherwise be. These balancing organs typically have the shape of a lollipop with the "stick" end attaching to the thorax. In some species, each haltere is tucked into a pouch, called a calyptere, that dips down from the forewing. Whatever their appearance, the halteres work the same way. Each has extremely touchy sensors that pick up even slight rotational movements, such as dips or rolls, and alert flight muscles to make the necessary adjustments to keep the fly from veering from its path.

All insects are wingless for at least part of their lives, yet they are usually fully capable of moving about on land, in the water, or underground. The wingless phase shared by all insects is their larval, or nymphal, form, whether it be a caterpillar or a grub that bears no resemblance to the adult or a nymph that can almost pass for a miniature adult. The mayfly is the only insect that has wings for any part of its larval development, for just a brief period immediately preceding its final metamorphosis into an adult.

On land, larvae and adult insects make their way around in numerous ways, including leaping, walking and/or running, and inching along.

Step by Step

If all of a sudden you had six legs sprouting from your chest instead of the two now off your abdomen, how would you walk? Would you try to step with the front pair, then the second, and finally the last two? Would you attempt to move the three legs on each side together, and alternate from side to side? When an insect walks, it keeps one foot of each pair on the ground, and does not raise any of the front four feet until the foot immediately behind it is firmly situated. In other words, at least three feet—a tripod of two on one side and one on the other—are always supporting the insect. Some insects veer from this pattern a bit. Mantids, for example, lift both front legs at once in their attack-defense stance. For most insects, however, the tripod support and alternate leg movements provide a stable base while they walk. Jumping, however, is another story.

Leaps and Bounds

A grasshopper's leaping ability is indeed amazing. A typical grass-hopper can jump about 20 times its body length. For a five-foot-tall (1.5 m) person to do the same, he or she would have to bound 100 feet (30.5 m), or a third of the way down a football field, in a single leap. Even when taking a running approach,

Olympic athletes can only muster about 23 to 29.5 feet (7–9 m). How does the grasshopper manage its stupendous leaps from a standing start?

Grasshoppers are such accomplished jumpers in part because they do not merely rely on their muscles—although their hind legs have considerable muscle tissue inside. They also depend on a locking system that keeps the legs in a high-strung position until they are released and the legs instantaneously thrust out and give a powerful boost to the insect's vault.

Even more impressive jumpers are the tiny fleas. Although they range from just 0.04 to 0.31 inches (1–8 mm) in length, they can leap amazing distances. Even the smallest fleas can make jumps of four to five inches (10.2–12.7 cm), and some can bound nearly 200 times their body length.

Inching Along

Caterpillars have a series of fleshy tubes, called prolegs, lying along and toward the rear of the body. The prolegs have a similar function to the three pairs of true legs that they have on the first three segments. With its legs, the muscles in its body, and pressure exerted by "blood" pressure, a caterpillar moves the front part of the body forward, and the prolegs follow behind. The effect is a slight

lengthening and shortening of the body as the caterpillar progresses.

In certain species, especially in caterpillars of moths in the family Geometridae, the abdomen has only a few prolegs, and all of them are at the end of the body. Without any prolegs in the middle, the rear ones have to repeatedly catch up with the front end. This lifts the center of the body well above the ground into an upside-down U shape until the front legs again walk forward and the body flattens back out. Among these caterpillars, the front, true legs can let go of the substrate completely while they seek a new point of purchase, leaving the larva attached only by its rear prolegs. This unusual movement is reflected in the common names of inchworms and loopers.

Left: The inchworm is a type of caterpillar that moves forward with the three pairs of true legs located toward the head of its body. As it does, other leglike structures, called prolegs, at the rear of the body run to catch up, pushing the center of the body into an upside-down U shape.

Opposite page top: With the exception of mayflies, only adult insects have working flight wings. Young grasshoppers have small, but nonfunctional, wing pads and must get around by walking or leaping until they become adults.

Opposite page bottom: Praying mantids, such as this one from India, are unlike most other insects in the way that they support themselves. Most insects hold at least one leg from each pair to the ground at all times, but praying mantids often raise both front legs, using them much as humans use their arms.

Buried Treasures

Although we may not always be aware of them, insects are squirming below our feet, scrabbling in the walls, scraping inside tree trunks, and squeezing between the top and bottom sides of a leaf. These include the ants and other soil tunnelers, along with various wood borers and leaf miners.

Dirt Dwellers

A multitude of creatures live in the leaf litter and soil below. Many of them are minute organisms, including springtails and other often-minute, wingless varieties with names such as springtail, telsontail or conehead, bristletail, silverfish, and firebrat. Many scientists now consider springtails and telsontails to be insectlike, but not really insects. Part of the reason is that a springtail has fewer segments in its abdomen than a "true" insect, and a telsontail has one too many.

Wood Borers

A large number of beetle grubs are perfectly content in the soil, but others prefer an existence within wood. One is the larva of a long-horned beetle, which includes several species in the genus *Monochamus*. These larvae, called pine sawyers, noisily chomp away inside pine trees. They can be so loud that campers on an otherwise-quiet night often report hearing the grubs' scraping.

Another common wood borer is the larder beetle (*Dermestes lardarius*). Most people become aware of this one-third to one-half-inch (0.8–1.3 cm) or smaller oval beetle when they see it crawling across the floor in their homes. Adults feed on all sorts of things, including carpets, leather products, dead flies and other insects, and food stored in a pantry or larder. Their

Below left: Although they may be more familiar to most people from a damp bathroom or basement, the wingless insects called silverfish are typically found outdoors in leaf litter or soil.

Below right: The bark of this fir tree shows the telltale signs of a bark beetle infestation. Female wood-boring beetles typically make an initial tunnel, or gallery, where they lay their eggs, and the hatching grubs continue the tunneling. Infestations are sometimes fatal to trees.

wood-boring phase occurs as the beetle grubs prepare to pupate. At this time, the larvae may make minute tunnels into wood, as well as cork and some types of insulation.

Leaf Miners

The random-looking squiggles or brown patches commonly found on leaf surfaces may be evidence of leaf-mining activities by the insect larvae of flies, butterflies and moths, beetles, and sawflies. Incredible as it may seem, the larvae are so minuscule that they can feed on—and survive on—the tissue and sap they find between the top and bottom layers of a leaf.

The sawflies are typical miners. Related to bees and wasps, the sawflies look much like wasps as adults. Not all of them mine leaves, but many do. As might be expected, the leaf-mining sawflies are small even as adults, usually growing to only 0.08 inches (0.2 cm) long at most. The females lay their eggs on or in the leaves of certain plants or trees. Sometimes, they are extremely particular and will only lay their eggs on certain species of tree. When the eggs hatch, the larvae move into leaves, sometimes more than one larva to a leaf. They frequently have angled or pointed heads to help them wedge their way through the leaf's interior. Some of the larvae stay inside the leaf until they are ready to pupate, but others emerge early and do some feeding outside until they pupate.

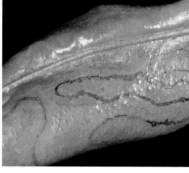

Above: The lesions caused by a leaf-mining insect are clearly visible in the brown squiggles on this leaf. Tiny insect larvae squeeze between the upper and lower surfaces of a leaf and eat the plant tissue and sap that they find there.

Below left: Ants typically have claws on their feet to help them cling to branches, whether they are right-side up or upside down.

CLIMBING THE WALLS

Part of the reason that bees and ants can scale vertical surfaces is their claws, which are able to find and use tiny footholds on rough walls. When the wall is too slick, they have another tactic. Sticky pads emerge from between the claws and adhere to the wall. According to a team of German and American researchers, these insects can release and extend the pads on each foot at will, so a foot may either stick and hold the insect in place, or let go so that it can take a step.

Water Lovers

In their habitat, aquatic insects may walk underwater, paddle through it, do a backstroke, or walk on top of the surface. In perhaps the most unusual form of water-borne locomotion, one type of insect can even get around by using its anus for jet propulsion.

Swimmers

Giant water bugs (of the family Belostomatidae) are one group of aquatic insects that paddle their way through the water. The large bugs swim by paddling their flattened middle and hind legs. Some predacious diving

In typical water strider fashion, this freshwater species holds its front pair of legs out of the water while skating along the surface with its middle and rear pairs. Some strider species are marine organisms and skitter along the surface of near-shore ocean waters.

beetles (family Dytiscidae) perform more of a forward freestyle stroke to traverse the water, while the back-swimmers (true bugs in the family Notonectidae) use their oarlike hind legs to propel them along as they lie floating on their backs. All of these swimmers need air to breathe. The giant water bug takes in its oxygen by swimming to the surface and poking up two snorkel-like tubes to draw in air. The diving beetles and backswimmers, on the other hand, are not so much snorkelers as they are scuba divers. A diving beetle's "tanks" are little bubbles of air it traps below its hardened fore-wings, and those of a backswimmer are air pockets it captures among small hairs on the bottom of its body.

Walking on Water

Water striders (a true bug in the family Gerridae) walk not under the water, but on top of it. With four of their legs, they walk, or more accurately skate, on the surface, while keeping the front pair held up and available for catching prey. To a very light insect such as the water strider, the surface tension of still water combines with the waterproof hairs on its body and legs to keep it afloat. According to researchers at the Massachusetts Institute of Technology, a water strider is even able to climb up slippery, liquid slopes, such as those that occur where the water abuts a rock of the shoreline. The slopes may seem minuscule from the human perspective, but they can be twice as tall as the strider. To do it, the scientists found, the insect presses down with its middle legs to make small dimples in the surface, and then pulls itself up the slope with claws on its front and hind legs.

Fanny Pack

A larval dragonfly has little in common with its parents. It looks nothing like them, and it lives underwater. The larva, called a naiad or aquatic nymph, usually walks or swishes its tail to navigate the area in search of something to eat. Occasionally, however, it needs to make a quick getaway from one of its own predators, and it has a outstanding defensive method for just that purpose. The naiad crunches its legs up against its body, sucks water through its anus into a chamber just inside the body, and then jets the water back through the anus in a strong stream that powers the naiad away. The action only sends the insect a few inches, but the sudden movement is often startling enough to drive off the predator.

Even if the predator is undaunted, the sudden movement often stirs up sufficient sediment to hide the naiad's escape.

This underwater-living, immature dragonfly, called a naiad, can make an emergency getaway by forcing a burst of water out of its anus. The jet not only quickly propels the insect a short distance, but can also stir up sand and muck to hide its escape.

TAILING A BEE

Bees are busy little creatures that speedily fly from place to place, often in dizzying paths that take them in and out of weedy tangles and between stems and flowers. For scientists who wanted to study individual bee's movements in the past, this presented real obstacles. Today, however, researchers have the option of using a specially designed radar system capable of tracking a single bee, provided the insect has been outfitted with a tiny backpacklike device that picks up the radar signal and transmits it back. Similar equipment is now in use for following the movements of other individual insects, including butterflies and beetles.

This bee is flying under the radar, but scientists are outfitting other bees, butterflies, and beetles with devices to track their movements.

CHAPTER 9

WHAT'S ON THE MENU

A VISIT TO A BACKYARD VEGETABLE GARDEN can provide a glimpse into the diversity of insect feeding habits. Bees, flies, and butterflies move from one flower to the next and use their long, strawlike mouthparts to extract nectar and sometimes pollen. Tomato hornworms (*Manduca quinquemaculata*) may work their chewing jaws to nibble the leaves from a tomato or pepper plant. These plump, white-striped, green moth caterpillars grow to 3 or 4 inches (7.6–10.2 cm) long. Gardeners may unknowingly see evidence of another insect's feeding activity when they spy a hornworn covered in "eggs." These are actually cocoons of a parasitic wasp in the family Braconidae. The female lays her eggs in the caterpillar, and the eggs hatch into larvae that eat the caterpillar's body tissues until they pupate as the "eggs" that cling to the outside of the hornworm's body. As well as these more obvious insects, many others, including the surface-dwelling and underground decomposers, are busy dining elsewhere in the garden. A few of them, including various beetles, even consume these decomposers. The following pages will explore some of the chewing, blood-sucking, liquid-sponging, and even human body–eating insects with which we share our world.

Left: Insect pests may have pests of their own. This caterpillar, for example, known to gardeners as a tomato hornworm, is covered with eggs laid by a parasitic wasp. When the eggs hatch, the wasp larvae will consume the hornworm. Inset: Many bees, flies, and butterflies extract nectar from flowers. Rather than keeping the nectar for itself, this honey bee will carry the liquid back to the hive, where it will be made into honey.

Chewing Insects

Above: Chewing insects, such as this long-horned beetle in the family Cerambycidae, have jaws set sideways on the head, rather than one jaw on top of the other as humans do. Insect chewing, therefore, is a side-to-side motion.

Below right: Dragonflies are highly effective predators capable of capturing prey on the wing. This male eastern pondhawk (*Erythemis simplicicollis*) has nabbed and is eating a moth. Female eastern pondhawks are bright green.

The mouth of an insect has little in common with a human's. Even among the insects that bite their food with a pair of jaws as we do, numerous differences exist. A chewing insect's jaws are situated sideways on the head rather than one above the other, so that they clamp together from side to side, as an elevator door would shut. We have upper and lower lips, but insects have an upper flap called a labrum that covers the vertical slit between the two jaws and a lower "lip" flap, the labium. Other features that set insects apart are four short tentacles called palpi—two on the "lower lip" and two nearby—that have the primary job of sensing whether an item is edible.

Midair Meals

The side-to-side chewing motion of the jaws is especially evident in a typical dragonfly, which will bite at nearly anything held against its mouth, including a prodding human finger. Fortunately, though a dragonfly's jaws are powerful enough to dismantle another insect, they usually cannot break the skin of a person's digit.

A skillful and swift flier, a dragonfly will prey on a variety of flying insects, often using its spiny forelegs to snap the prey out of midair. Often, this hunter will settle on a branch or stem, hold its captured prey in its forelegs, and bite off chunk after chunk until everything is gone but the wings, which it lets drop away.

Aquatic Nabbers

Even as a youngster, a dragonfly is a proficient predator. After hatching and before becoming a winged adult, a dragonfly lives underwater as a wingless naiad with an extraordinary weapon for capturing prey, including

tadpoles and small fish that may be bigger than the naiad. The weapon is an especially large labium, a jointed structure that with blinding speed can fling out as its palpi grab hold of the prey and pull the startled victim back to its waiting jaws.

Skin Eaters

Members of one beetle family (Dermestidae) are so adept at chewing that museums use them to clean the meat off carcasses for their skeleton collections. One commonly used beetle is the appropriately named hide beetle (*Dermestes maculatus*). Both the 0.2- to 0.4-inch-long (5–10 mm) brown to black adult beetles and their larvae will eat skin, tissue, and any other protein-laden food they can find—alive or recently departed. Some museums start their colonies of hide beetles by finding roadkill, plucking the beetles from it, and tossing them along with the body of a dead animal into a sealed box. Soon, the beetles begin procreating and a full colony is formed. Once it reaches sufficient size, perhaps a few hundred beetles and larvae, the colony requires only a matter of three or four days to completely scour the skull of a large mammal, such as a wolf or a bear. They may also infect houses when a squirrel or mouse has died in the chimney or walls.

Although they are in the same order, Odonata, dragonflies and damselflies can be easily distinguished from one another. One of their most obvious differences is the way they hold their wings when they are at rest: damselflies, such as the one pictured here, hold them closed together, and dragonflies keep them spread apart.

SPECIFICATIONS

Insects: Dragonflies and damselflies
Order: Odonata
Meaning of Odonata: "toothed jaw," referring to its mouthparts
Typical characteristics of adults in this order:
- two pair of large, long, and membranous similarly sized wings that cannot be folded down over the body
- long, often-slender abdomen
- a maneuverable head that can rotate from side to side
- two ample, bulging, compound eyes that may cover much of the head
- very short antennae
- biting, toothed mouthparts
- eggs that hatch into aquatic nymphs, or naiads, that look considerably different from adults

DIVERSITY
Number of known species: about 5,500
Size: Two of the smallest members of the order are the scarlet dwarf (*Nannophya pygmaea*) of Southeast Asia and Australia, and another closely related species known by the scientific name of *Nannophyopsis chalcosoma*. These dragonflies measure about 0.6 inches (1.5 cm) long and have a wingspan of 0.75 inches (1.7–2 cm). The largest is a damselfly known by the scientific name of *Megaloprepus coerulatus* of Central America. This enormous insect has a body 4.7 inches (12 cm) long and a wingspan of up to 7.5 inches (19 cm).
Sampling of benefits to humans: The naiads, especially, serve as food for fish and other aquatic organisms, and the adults are voracious predators of pest insects, such as mosquitoes. Dragonflies also have cultural significance in many areas of the world.

Piercing, Sucking Insects

Anyone who spends time outdoors on a summer evening knows too well about the mouthparts of insects, such as mosquitoes and tiny midges known as no-see-ums or punkies. Humans and other animals, however, are not the only victims of piercing, sucking insects. Many members of this group also slice instead into plant tissues for their meals.

Mosquitoes

The mosquitoes that are such an annoyance to humans are actually just good mothers. While the males are off feeding on plant sap, the females are risking life and limb to get the protein from our blood for the eggs developing inside their bodies. Whether they are after nectar or blood, both sexes have a tubelike mouth, the proboscis, that acts as a straw. The female's proboscis,

This milkweed bug is a member of the seed bug family, Lygaeidae, and feeds on milkweed plants. When a true bug finds a prey-worthy plant or animal, it draws forth a long snout that it otherwise holds flat against its underside. It then injects digestive juices into the prey, and sucks up the partially processed tissues.

BLOOD, SWEAT, AND TEARS
Blood, sweat, and tears—maybe a mosquito bite is not enough to cause tears, but the insect does follow the scent of sweat to find a human victim and draw blood. Researchers now know at least one thing that makes sweat so alluring. Female mosquitoes have an odor receptor that is sensitive to one of the molecules, a protein, in sweat, according to 2004 research at Yale University. The molecule is called 4-methylphenol. Besides this method of finding bite-worthy subjects, mosquitoes also home in on humans in other ways, including the carbon dioxide we exhale.

however, has serrated edges to slice into the skin. An extremely patient person can watch the process as his or her blood slowly fills and distends the female mosquito's body. If the female escapes the encounter unscathed, that single bloodletting may be all she needs to nourish her eggs until they hatch.

No-see-ums

Just like the mosquitoes, the tiny no-see-ums are a type of fly, the females of which require the protein from blood for their developing eggs. The typical mosquito gets its blood from a bird or a mammal, but the no-see-ums cast a wider net. They will bite other insects and are not above stealing from a female mosquito's belly, when they are not after humans.

Making Soup

True bugs in the order Hemiptera are some of the insects with piercing, sucking mouthparts. They have long, stabbing snouts with a tube inside. They can use the tube to deliver digestive juices into a plant or an animal prey to begin breaking down its tissues and later to suck up the soup of partially processed tissues. Depending on the insect's diet, the digestive juices may have an added kick. Although seed bugs (family Lygaeidae) need only to start dissolving the contents of seeds, predacious assassin bugs use their digestive juices to paralyze their insect prey before beginning the predigestion process.

Bedbugs

One of the true bugs that bites humans is the bedbug. The common bedbug (*Cimex lectularius*) is one of several bedbug species, and not only the females, but also the males and the nymphs, are bloodthirsty. As adults, the tiny oval insects are usually dark red to brown and about 0.2 inches (0.5 cm) long. The nymphs, which have the same dagger of a beak as their parents, can be as small as 0.04 inches (0.1 cm) long. Typically, bedbugs draw their blood at night, creeping out of mattresses, carpets, minuscule cracks in walls, and other concealed spots to feast on sleeping humans. The bites are

painless, and victims typically have no clue that they have been targeted until they see little spots of blood on their sheets or they perhaps begin to itch a day or two later. The itch is the human body's reaction to bedbug saliva. The saliva of mosquitoes and no-see-ums produces the same symptom. The insects inject the saliva to keep the blood flowing while they are feeding.

Below left: When it comes to bedbugs, the females are not alone in their bloodthirsty habits. Males and nymphs also have a taste for blood and will bite humans. Infestations of the common bedbug (*Cimex lectularius*), shown here, have become increasingly widespread in the United States.

Below: Only female mosquitoes "bite" and draw blood, and they do it to get protein for their developing eggs. Usually, this is merely an annoyance for humans, but the bites of some species can transmit disease.

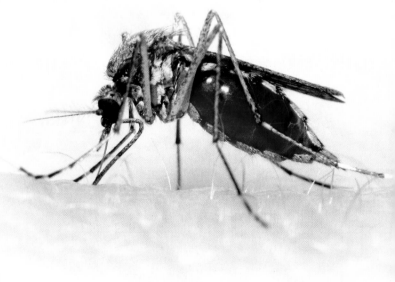

Nectar Sippers

Above: A careful look at this giant swallowtail (*Papilio cresphontes*) reveals that the proboscis is actually made up of two side-by-side feeding tubes.

Below: As this honey bee pokes into the flower for its nectar, the minute hairs on her body either pick up grains of pollen from the flower or deliver pollen from another flower.

Just as most animals reproduce by adding sperm from a male to an egg from a female, the majority of plants propagate by combining the pollen (the sperm) from one flower with the ovule (egg) within another. Therein lies the rub. Plants are nonmotile; they therefore need help with the pollination process. For many, insects are the pollen-movers, but what do they get out of the deal? The answer is nectar.

Pollination

When an insect visits a plant, it usually has to probe deep into the flower to reach the sweet, liquid nectar stored inside, and in so doing brushes past both the pollen-containing parts (the anthers) and the end of the hollow tube (the stigma) that leads to the ovule.

By moving between plants, the insect transfers pollen from one flower to the stigma of the next, facilitating cross-pollination. The insect gets a meal, and the plant eventually gains a fertilized ovule, commonly known as a seed.

Bees

Important pollinators, bees reach nectar with a sucking tube that generally extends a few millimeters beyond the head. Usually, a bee also has to push well into a flower, burying its head and part of its body in the flower to reach the sugary liquid. Some flowers have shapes that make a bee's retreat difficult. As the bee squirms to leave the flower, it picks up or drops off more pollen. Bees also collect pollen, which is a good source of protein for their larvae. Consequently, some flowers such as wild roses produce extra pollen, enough to pollinate other roses and to feed the bees. This occasionally backfires. Bees can become so firmly trapped in certain flowers, such as those of common milkweed (*Asclepias syriaca*), that they cannot escape at all and sometimes die there.

Butterflies and Moths

Adult butterflies and moths handle food gathering a bit differently. Each of these insect groups has a long proboscis formed by a pair of feeding tubes, sometimes extending as long as the entire body length. This proboscis easily reaches deep nectar stores. When not in use, it coils up under the head.

SNEAK PEEK

Bumblebees from one colony sneak peeks at feeding bumblebees from another, and then alter their own foraging strategy to copy that of the other bees, according to 2005 research at the University of Arizona. Scientists tested the insects' behavior by placing a living or fake model bumblebee on a fake flower. Afterward, they noted that spying bees started visiting similar flowers. When the model was moved to a different-colored flower, the spies changed gears, too. The copycat behavior was strong enough to compel the bees to visit flowers with colors they would ordinarily ignore in the wild.

Not all adult butterflies and moths use the proboscis for nectar. Members of the brush-footed butterfly family (Nymphalidae) are equal-opportunity sippers and will poke their proboscis into flowers for nectar, but will also plunge into tree sap and less-savory buffets, such as rotting fruit and animal scat. An example of a butterfly in this family is the mourning cloak (*Nymphalis antiopa*), a 2.5- to 3.5-inch (6.4–8.9 cm) butterfly common to forests of North America. The undersides of its wings are shades of brown and gray and have the pattern of tree bark. The upper surfaces of the wings, however, are chocolate brown trimmed in indigo spots and edged in pale gold. This insect is one of the first butterflies out and about after a long, cold winter. With few flowers available, it instead gets its nutrition in early spring from the sap flowing from wounds in trees. Later in the year, people commonly see it sipping at rotting fruit.

Heliconius butterflies (Nymphalidae) are unusual because they collect pollen and then retain it on the proboscis until it germinates. This releases the pollen's proteins, which feed the butterfly. This diet allows them to live as adults for up to five months. Most other butterflies live as adults for only a week or two. Some adult butterflies and moths have no mouthparts at all. These live only a few days, just long enough to mate and start the next generation.

Above: The somber colors of the mourning cloak butterfly (*Nymphalis antiopa*) are enlivened by a band of lustery gold. Although the mourning cloak will sip nectar, it generally feeds on tree sap.

Background: Bumblebees investigate purple flowers. Studies have shown that bumblebees follow cues from other bumblebees when choosing a flower on which to feed.

The long-living *Heliconius charitonius*, or zebra longwing, feasts on both nectar and pollen.

Spongers

Above: An extreme close-up of *Musca domestica*—otherwise known as the common housefly.

Below right: The bush fly (*Musca vetustissima*) may pick up nutrition from a steaming pile of animal dung and then zero in on the damp corner of a person's mouth or a teary eye. As expected, this behavior can lead to nasty human infections, one of which can cause blindness.

Along with mosquitoes and no-see-ums, there are other flies that have piercing, sucking mouthparts. These include the pesky female deerflies that fly circles around a hiker's head only to periodically land and take a bite. A good number of flies do not bite into flesh, however, but they have some other unpleasant characteristics.

Houseflies

The mouth of a common housefly (*Musca domestica*) is mainly a proboscis, sometimes called a rostrum, with two short palpi about halfway down and a fleshy pad at the end. The pad absorbs fluids and picks up bits of solid food, and the fly sucks up both through the proboscis. Houseflies can also distinguish between possible food items with their feet, which carry sensory hairs. Although this ability would suggest that they are choosy about their diet, flies have widely varying tastes. This characteristic can pose threats to human health. For example, a fly may spend a few minutes lunching on an animal carcass or a pile of fresh dung before dropping in to sponge up a drop of soda on an opened soft-drink can or a bit of juice on a newly bitten apple. As well as taking nourishment from the soda and apple, it may leave behind disease-causing bacteria from a touch of their mouth or feet, or through their feces or vomit. Some of the bacteria can lead to typhoid, cholera, dysentery, or other diseases.

Bush Flies

A particularly bothersome and disgusting insect, the bush fly (*Musca vetustissima*) closely resembles a housefly and often lives around animals on ranches or farms. This insect seeks out moist things associated with both humans and other animals. It may

To a blowfly, nothing gets the stomach growling like the smell of rotting flesh. Although they usually gather on dead animals for supper, they will occasionally add some variety with a stop at a carrion-scented flower.

land on and attempt to gather some nutrition from wet corners of a person's mouth, tearing eyes, and runny nose, as well as a festering wound on an animal or a pile of still-damp scat. When they travel from the latter to the former, the possibility for human infection escalates. They are one of the insects that can cause trachoma, an eye infection that, untreated, can lead to blindness.

Blowflies

Blowflies (family Calliphoridae) are primarily carrion feeders. Occasionally they will also visit a flower, but only those that smell like putrid meat. One of the plants that at least partially relies on the flies for pollination is skunk cabbage (*Symplocarpus foetidus*). It is among the first plants to flower in the spring, sometimes bursting through the snow. Its tiny, light-yellow flowers are set on an oval knob and housed in a purplish cup that may be several inches tall and looks somewhat like the claw of a lobster. Another rotten meat–scented flower that draws blowflies is that of the American pawpaw (*Asimina triloba*), a tree with a soft, edible fruit. The flowers, which bloom in the spring, are reddish purple and about 2 inches (5.1 cm) long. With leaves that can reach about a foot (30.5 cm) long, however, the flowers are not especially obvious. Commercial pawpaw farmers sometimes encourage flies to visit the blooms on their crop by hanging roadkill from tree branches.

Food Farmers

Ants have been farming for millions of years, long before humans developed the practice. The insects may not have rows of corn and tomatoes, but some ants nonetheless grow all of their own food and carefully tend their gardens.

Leafcutter Ants

Leafcutter ants (in the genus *Atta*) snip off bits of leaves, often much larger than the individual ants and up to 20 times heavier, hoist them above their heads, and haul them back to the nest. They will also cart plant and tree buds to the nest. There, they chew the leaves and buds, but they do not eat them. Instead, they use the macerated vegetation as fertilizer on and around a garden of fungus, which serves as the sole food source for the entire colony.

Fungus Starter

The fungus garden of the Texas leafcutter ant, also known as the parasol ant (*Atta texanus*), gets its start from a small clump of fungus a newly mature queen ant steals from her parent colony before she sets off to begin her own. When she finds a suitable underground spot, she spits out the clump, uses her waste products to boost its growth, and then starts to lay eggs. Rather than dining on the still-small fungus patch, she eats a number of her own eggs to survive, but lets some hatch into larvae and grow into worker ants. These ants take on the leaf-cutting and bud-collecting chores to enlarge the garden, which soon becomes large enough to feed the queen, the workers, and the new larvae. Eventually, a single nest of Texas leafcutter ants may contain more than two million ants and extend 20 feet (6.1 m) into the ground.

Below left: Leafcutter ants, like these from the Amazon region of South America, can carry leaves up to 20 times their body weight.

Below right: A leafcutter ant hauls a leaf along a path in the Soberanía National Park in Panama.

A colony of leafcutter ants (*Atta cephalotes*) in Monteverde, Costa Rica, hover over and tend to eggs, larvae, and pupae lying atop a garden of fungus.

Tending the Garden

As well as fertilizing their garden, some leafcutter ants tend it by weeding out invasive fungus, along with tiny, foreign fungus spores. Scientists from the University of Texas at Austin and New Zealand's University of Otago discovered this by spraying spore-containing water on the fungus garden of a colony of Panamanian leafcutter ants (*Atta colombica*). The ants quickly recognized the foreign spores and speedily moved in to pull off the spores by running strands of fungus through their mouthparts. If a piece of macerated leaf was too infected to salvage, they would take it out of the garden and remove it from the nest. Introduced bits of foreign fungus met the same fate. The ants would immediately carry it outside for disposal.

Codependence

For many years, scientists thought that the fungus needed the ants as much as the ants needed the fungus. The fungus, it was believed, reproduced and dispersed only through new sprouts from an existing growth rather than by spores, as most fungi do. Recently, however, scientists at the University of Texas and Tennessee's Vanderbilt University found that the fungus is fully capable of spreading out and propagating via spores and can survive even in the absence of the ants. The ants, however, still depend solely on the fungus for their food, and they need their farming skills to survive.

MAN-MADE INSECTS?

Urban legend has it that the multitude of lovebugs (*Plecia nearctica*) that splatter across windshields in the southern United States are escapees from a University of Florida experiment that attempted to genetically engineer the insect for mosquito control. The man-made bugs would breed with male mosquitoes and produce sterile offspring and at the same time keep the males from mating with female mosquitoes. It is a great story, but it is false. The lovebug, which is actually a small black fly with a red thorax, is a nature-created insect that expanded its range from Central America into Mexico and the southern United States during the last century. The flies congregate in enormous numbers for mating in the spring and male-female pairs frequently remain connected abdomen to abdomen for hours, giving them their other common name: two-headed bugs. Although motorists may curse the insects, they do have an important function: their larvae scarf up rotting leaves and are therefore important decomposers.

Swarms

In Keren, Ethiopia, a man walks through a swarm of desert locusts. Plagues of locusts have threatened agricultural production in North Africa for centuries. The voracious insects threaten the food supply because they eat so much of the area's vegetation during an invasion.

A single grasshopper may nibble a few leaves from a plant on a given day, and a couple dozen grasshoppers on the same plant can cause considerable damage. What happens then when millions of the insects converge and go on a feeding frenzy?

Huge Swarms

A plague of grasshoppers occurs somewhere on Earth at least once a year. In 2004 and 2005, for example, large and thick swarms of 2- to 3-inch-long (5.1–7.6 cm) and sometimes longer grasshoppers, called desert locusts (*Schistocerca gregaria*), started their march. This mass movement blanketed parts of West Africa, scouring the land of plant life and leaving hundreds of thousands of people with little to eat. Experts said that these two plagues were the worst ones since at least 15 years earlier, when the area experienced another band of locust infestations.

Damage from locust swarms is not limited to Africa. Settlers in the Great Plains of the United States met up with the Rocky Mountain locust (*Melanoplus spretus*) in the 1800s. These locusts, usually ranging from about 0.8 to 1.4 inches (2–3.5 cm) in body length, formed a thick cloud that stretched from the ground into the sky, where it blocked out the sun. According

This single desert locust (*Schistocerca gregaria*) at the Bristol Zoo in England looks completely innocuous. When its species swarms, however, the insects can fill the sky and the ground and devour many acres of vegetation, including entire farm fields.

to reports of the day, one mammoth swarm of the locusts covered an area nearly the size of both Wyoming and Colorado. The insects cleared the land of all vegetation and gnawed away at anything potentially edible, including the wooden handles on hoes and the leather on saddles.

And Then There Were None

Despite the immensity of the Rocky Mountain locust swarms in America's Great Plains, all of the insects disappeared by the beginning of the twentieth century, never to be seen again. Many scientists now believe that the locusts died out when their permanent home—the area where they live their solo lives between forays in swarms—vanished to habitat destruction caused by mining and farming operations. Some researchers, however, suspect that some individual Rocky Mountain locusts may still survive here and there. If so, the possibility of future swarms cannot be completely discounted.

Why Swarm?

With so many insects crowding together and vying for the same resources, what is the benefit of swarming? Scientists at the University of North Carolina studied the question by looking at Mormon crickets (*Anabrus simplex*) and reported their results in 2006.

These rather chubby-looking, flightless crickets gather by the millions to trek together across the land. The researchers captured some of the swarming insects, attached transmitters to their bodies, set them free, and followed them. The experiments showed that crickets remaining within the band were still alive two days later, but 50 to 60 percent of those that struck out on their own fell victim to predators. Apparently, being part of the crowd, even if it means having to fight for food, is a better survival tactic than breaking ranks.

Other researchers have pondered the trigger that sets off the swarms in the first place. Among the desert locusts, the stimulus is population density. Crowded locusts begin to brush against one another, and their legs are particularly sensitive to this jostling. According to 2004 research at the University of Leicester in the United Kingdom, just four hours of leg nudging can cause a locust to prepare to swarm.

Using Mormon crickets (*Anabrus simplex*), such as these photographed in Nevada, scientists have begun weighing the pros and cons for the crickets remaining within a swarm and vying with many others for a limited food source, or striking out on the path less taken.

CHAPTER 10

CREATURE COMFORTS

LARGE OR SMALL, DIRECT OR INDIRECT, the overall contributions insects make to life on Earth are beyond measure. Caddisflies, stoneflies, and other insects serve as bioindicators, measuring the health of aquatic ecosystems. Lovebugs, fly maggots, and dermestid beetles are just a few of the six-legged decomposers that help clear away the waste products, rotting leaves, and dead bodies of animals that would otherwise quickly cover our planet. This cleanup role also fertilizes the soil, making it a better nursery for seeds and seedlings and a richer ground for already-established plants and trees that generate a significant portion of breathable air. Insects benefit plants even further. Many flowering plants, including a high percentage of agricultural crops, depend on insect pollination. In addition, insects are a vital link in the food web, as predators of creatures and plants and also as prey for all manner of fishes, birds, mammals, amphibians, and reptiles. It would be difficult, if not impossible, to find a single human food item that does not have some connection to insects. Occasionally, those ties are straightforward. People of certain cultures intentionally eat insects, some of which are considered delicacies, and people worldwide savor bee-made honey. Some people even wear clothing made out of an insect product.

Left: A leaping frog prepares to make a meal of a damselfly. This damselfly, an ebony jewelwing (*Calopteryx maculata*), has likely been a predator itself. Its diet includes small insects, such as gnats and aphids. Inset: Insects may not be typical restaurant fare, but people in many cultures would find this plate of maggots to be a welcome addition to their daily menu.

Insect-Flower, Inc.

Flowering plants can reproduce in only a few ways. Some can send up shoots straight from a parent plant's roots or rhizomes (underground stems). Some can self-pollinate, which means that the plant's pollen can fall onto and fertilize its own developing seed, or ovule. For many plants, however, their only option is cross-pollination: the pollen from one plant must travel by wind, water, or animal transportation to the ovule of another to fertilize it. Among all of these methods, insects rule. Estimates suggest that they are responsible for 65 to 80 percent of the cross-pollination of all flowering plants on the planet.

Right: Unlike most butterflies, which consume only nectar, the crimson-patched longwing butterfly (*Heliconius erato*) will also eat pollen. When this butterfly is collecting pollen, it runs its proboscis over the flower's pollen-covered anthers rather than probing deep into the flower for nectar.

Below: From a human's vantage point, a flower's pollen may look like dust. This photo, magnified about 500 times, shows pollen from common plants, such as sunflower (*Helianthus annuus*), morning glory (*Ipomoea purpurea*), prairie hollyhock (*Sildalcea malviflora*), golden-rayed lily (*Lilium auratum*), sundrops primrose (*Oenothera fruticosa*), and castor bean (*Ricinus communis*).

Nectar and Pollen

For many insects, a flower's sugary nectar is the reward and their brushes with pollen are purely inadvertent. Some insects, however, eat pollen. One reason is the amino acids in the pollen. Amino acids are the chemical compounds found in proteins. Although most adult butterflies are strictly nectar-feeders, the crimson-patched longwing (*Heliconius erato*) will consume pollen. The longwing, which lives in North, Central, and South America, has velvet-black wings, each of the front two with a broad red vertical band, and each of the hind pair with a single yellow horizontal stripe. The longwing uses some of the pollen as a nutrient to boost its egg production, but also transports some to the next flower.

Coevolution: Hand in Hand

Whether they are nectar or pollen aficionados—or both—insect pollinators are critical to the survival of many wildflowers, shrubs, and trees. Without them, tens of thousands of plant species would be unable to reproduce and would eventually become extinct. On the flip side, the elimination of flowering plants would mean the demise of a vast array of insects, many of which rely upon flowers for all of their food. This life-or-death connection links the two different organisms—plants and insects—so closely that many have evolved in concert. Scientists call the process coevolution. It occurs when a species' traits evolve to become at least partially dependent on the evolution of compatible traits in a genetically unrelated species to which it is somehow tied.

For example, a plant mutation may produce a slightly different color pattern on its flower petals that more effectively steers pollinating insects toward its nectar, much as lights and painted markings direct incoming jetliners to a runway. Pollen-using insects that have the ability to read those flower patterns correctly are rewarded with an easy-to-find nectar cache. In this case, the plant develops the pattern and the insect develops the ability to make sense of it. If, however, the plant is also visited by other insects that cannot detect and decipher the pattern, the plant will lose those pollinators. In that case, the insects will miss out on the nectar unless the plant of the insects—or both—are able to evolve better-matched characteristics. This is evident among

flowers, such as the blanketflower (*Gaillardia grandiflora*), which has bright-red coloration that attracts butterflies, as well as an ultraviolet hue that draws in bees, which are UV-sensitive but blind to red.

SEED-SOWING ANTS

About one of every three species of plant in the grassy habitat of South Africa known as fynbos has native ants to thank for its continued survival. The ants carry seeds into their nests and take small bites out of them, but leave enough of the seeds intact to sprout into new plants. Recently, this mutually beneficial arrangement that yields food for the ants and seed-sowing for the plants has hit a snag, according to a researcher at the University of California-Davis. Argentine ants (*Linepithema humile*) have moved into South Africa and are taking over habitat from some of the native ants. The invading ants sow no seeds, and experiments suggest ant-reliant plants in infested zones may be able to recover from a fire and sprout at only a tenth of the rate of plants in zones where the native ants still thrive.

Left: Some ants sow seeds by carrying them into their underground nests and leaving them there after they have taken a few nibbles. Although they look different, these two ants are likely the same species. The larger-headed one is a so-called soldier, and when necessary, it uses its massive jaws to defend the nest.

Background: The red bull's-eye pattern on this flower, known as a blanketflower or painted daisy (*Gaillardia grandiflora*), attracts butterflies, which can see it. Honey bees and other bees are blind to red, but they can see the flower's ultraviolet colors, which human eyes cannot detect.

Honey Secrets

Before you spoon honey into a cup of tea or spread it onto a biscuit, consider what honey is. Or better yet, blissfully ignore how a bee makes it: the sweet, syrupy concoction is nectar that has been ingested, regurgitated, taken into the mouths of other bees, spit out, and partially dehydrated.

The Process

The first step in honey production is the collection of nectar by a honey bee (*Apis mellifera*). The insect has a tube-shaped proboscis formed by part of the jaw and the labium; it uses the apparatus like a straw to suck the runny, liquid nectar into one of its stomachs. Honey bees have two organs called stomachs: one like ours that digests food, including some of the nectar they gather; and a second so-called honey stomach strictly for holding nectar temporarily. A bee must visit dozens, even hundreds of flowers before it can collect enough nectar to fill its honey stomach. A completely full honey stomach can weigh as much as the bee.

During its foraging trip or its return to the hive, the bee may force some of the nectar in its honey stomach back into its mouth, where it mixes the nectar with digestive enzymes. The job of the enzymes is to split the nectar's large sugar molecule, called sucrose, into two smaller sugar molecules, known as glucose and fructose. Back at the hive, the bee spits up all of the nectar from its honey stomach, and it and other bees continue to work on the regurgitated nectar by taking it into their moths to add additional enzymes and to remove water from it. Eventually, the nectar becomes increasingly concentrated, and when it is sufficiently gooey, it becomes honey. The bees store the honey in individual wax cells of their honeycomb and seal each cell with a wax cap.

Below left: This honey bee is collecting pollen and nectar from a sunflower. It sucks the nectar into its honey stomach before returning to the nest, where it regurgitates much of it back into its mouth, chews it, and then spits it out in the first steps of honey production.

Below right: Honey bees store the honey they make inside the hive's hexagonal wax cells. When a cell is full, the bees cap it with wax. Beekeepers monitor the hive and slice away capped sections to reap the sweet harvest.

The Harvest

Bees use their honey primarily to feed their growing larvae, and fortunately for humans, they make plenty extra. A typical hive of 40,000 bees may make double or triple the amount it needs, which leaves a bountiful harvest for a beekeeper. Beekeepers watch their hives and begin cutting away pieces of the hive after the bees have finished capping the cells. To prepare liquid honey for packaging, the beekeeper slices off the caps and places the now-oozing honeycomb in a centrifuge to quickly separate the comb from the honey. The honey may be amber, deep gold, or brown in color and may have different tastes. This variety can be traced to the species of flowers the bees visited while gathering nectar. In the United States, light-colored honey made from clover nectar is very popular, although U.S. consumers may also find regional honeys made from the nectar of avocados, blueberries, orange blossoms, and buckwheat. Tupelo honey, immortalized in a 1971 Van Morrison song, derives from the nectar of the Ogeeche tupelo (*Nyssa ogeche*). This red-fruited tree is native to northwestern Florida and the southern half of Georgia and produces what some people consider the best-tasting honey. Whichever nectar makes the tastiest honey, all of it is the result of considerable insect work. According to the Australian Honey Bee Industry Council, one pound of honey (450 grams), a typical jar size at a grocery store, represents about three weeks of foraging by 300 bees.

Above: Here, beekeepers check a portion of the hive, which the bees have constructed on an easily removable frame. The honey inside may have different colors or tastes, depending on the species of flowers from which the bees collected the nectar.

Left: A sealed jar of honey will keep indefinitely—even centuries, as evidenced by a find in an Egyptian tomb.

PERFECTLY PRESERVED

Honey never spoils. As long as it is not left open to absorb moisture from the air, it will keep for years. In fact, excavations of centuries-old Egyptian tombs have turned up perfectly good honey. This seemingly miraculous feat partially centers on honey's low water content, which is about 17 to 19 percent and too low for the growth of yeast that would spoil, or ferment, the honey. Recent research suggests that honey not only curtails yeast, but may also have a powerful effect on bacteria. Some hospitals in Australia have now begun using honey as an agent to fight antibiotic-resistant bacteria and help wounds heal.

The Web of Life

Both the adults and the larvae of this weevil and others in the family Belidae feed on plants. Adults have a long beak, or rostrum, with their jaws at the tip. The females of many species also use the rostrum to bore into plants and prepare a place to lay their eggs.

Without insects, humans would not last long on Earth. Although we could survive without honey, our diet would be heavily affected by the loss of many of the fruits and vegetables that depend on insect pollination. These losses, however, would only be the tip of the iceberg.

A Key Link

An important role for insects is to provide a link in the food chain, especially between the plants and the nonplant-eating animals. A simple, single food chain might look like this: A plant grows using energy from the sun and nutrients from the soil. An insect chomps the leaves of the plant. A bird devours the insect. A cat dines on the bird. Without the insect step, the chain falls apart because neither the bird nor the cat is a plant-eater. Of course, food chains are not as simple as this. Multiple chains overlap and intertwine to create an enormously complex food web. For instance, one plant may have dozens of insects that feed on it, each of the insects may have scores of predators (some of which may be other insects) and those predators may have many predators of their own.

With so many interconnections, we find it all too easy to lose track of the myriad, small players near the bottom of the web, and to focus on those at the top. Yet, like a house of cards, it is the bottom pieces, including the plant-eating insects, that form the foundation for everything above.

Where the Money Is

In recent years, many researchers as well as some commercial enterprises have begun taking a hard look at certain insects in the food web that might be effective in controlling various pest species. One is a weevil (the milfoil weevil, *Euhrychiopsis lecontei*) that has a taste for an aquatic plant called Eurasian milfoil (*Myriophyllum*

PESTICIDE MAKES POOR FORAGERS

Determining if a pesticide is safe for beneficial insects is a tricky business. A good measure is whether "good" insects die from exposure; but what if a dangerous effect is more subtle? Scientists at Simon Fraser University in British Columbia found in 2005 that pollen mixed with the pesticide spinosad was not fatal to bumblebee larvae (*Bombus impatiens*), but did cause them to grow into slow foragers. The adults noticeably contended with muscle tremors while trying to collect pollen and nectar from flowers. At first glance, this may seem to be of little importance, but because many plants depend on insects as their sole means of cross-pollination, widespread slowdowns have the potential to hinder plant reproduction.

This monarch cater-pillar prepares to enter pupation, the step before emerging as a butterfly.

CORN VERSUS BUTTERFLY

Does genetically engineered corn kill monarch butterfly caterpillars (*Danaus plexippus*)? The debate centers on Bt corn, which is typical corn except for an extra gene. This gene is from the bacterium known as *Bacillus thuringiensis*, and gives the corn the ability to make pesticide that kills its pests. Some research, including studies at Cornell University and Iowa State University, suggests the Bt corn pollen may waft onto other plants, where it deals a deadly blow to harmless species such as the monarch. Several other scientific papers, however, contain data showing only negligible impacts on monarchs from typical forms of Bt corn. So far, however, little to no research has delved into the effect of Bt crops on the wide range of other insects that may encounter the pesticide through corn pollen or other means, and the deliberations over this and further issues surrounding genetically modified food remain in full swing.

spicatum). Milfoil is an introduced plant in North America that came from either Europe, Asia, or both in the 1940s, possibly earlier, and is now a problem in inland lakes throughout the United States and parts of Canada. The plant grows densely and spreads quickly, forming thick mats that can greatly curtail recreational pursuits and affect the population of native plants and animals. Researchers have found that the milfoil weevil, a native species that measures only about 0.1 inches (3 mm) long, not only eats a native form of milfoil, but will also eat the introduced species. Several lake-management groups have since purchased weevils, and some lakes are now rebounding.

Some insects are popular for their carnivorous habits. Many companies, for instance, currently sell ladybird beetles (family Coccinellidae) to rein in aphids on houseplants and garden vegetation. Some also carry insects such as spined soldier bugs (*Podisus maculiventris*), praying mantids (including *Tenodera aridifolia*), and parasitic wasps (such as *Pediobius foveolatus* and *Aphidius matricariae*) to prey on garden and crop pests.

A number of gardening and other companies currently sell ladybird beetles, also known as ladybugs, as a pest-control measure for aphids. This black and cream-colored ladybird beetle is earning its keep by munching on a pea aphid.

Silk and Silkworms

Right: Silk producers collect the cocoons of *Bombyx mori* (shown here), and submerge them in boiling water until they begin to unravel into fine, long filaments. They then wind together several of the filaments to produce a length of silk thread for use in silk cloth.

Below: These silkworms, which are actually moth caterpillars, are eating their typical diet of mulberry leaves. Each will soon use glands in its mouth to spin its silken cocoon.

Silk dates back to around 2400 BCE, when according to legend, a Chinese empress was relaxing in the shade of a white mulberry (*Morus alba*), a tree with small, fleshy fruit and 3- to 6-inch-long (7.6–15.2 cm) leaves.

A white cocoon dropped from the tree into the hot tea she was drinking. Rather than quickly dumping the tea as most people would do, she watched as the cocoon started to unravel into a fine, lustrous filament, and got the idea that it could possibly be used to make a luxurious cloth. Her experiments with the filament, the story continues, led to silk-cloth production.

Legend aside, silk weaving did begin in China at about that time, and Chinese royalty draped themselves in the fabric. Soon it became all the rage among the extremely wealthy, who were the only ones who could afford it. China could command a high price because it cornered the market, refusing to reveal the process for making the product. The secret held for about three millennia before others in Japan, Korea, and Arabia discovered how to produce the thread. By the eleventh century, the skill had spread to Europe. Today, China and Japan are the major producers of high-quality, natural silk.

The Silkworm

The silkworm used commercially to make silk is not a worm, but a moth caterpillar (*Bombyx mori*). Like other moth caterpillars, it spins silk for its cocoon from glands in its mouth. When it first oozes from the glands, the silk is a thick, transparent liquid, but it hardens almost immediately into a glossy and fine-bur strong fiber. When the silkworm spins its cocoon, the 3-inch-long (7.6 cm) caterpillar uses one continuous thread of silk. By the time it has completed its task, the thread is usually around 1,500 to 3,000 feet (457–914 m) in length, long enough to reach from the sidewalk to the top of 15- to 30-story building. The larva pupates inside the cocoon for 14 to 21 days, and emerges as a moth with brown-mottled white wings that span about 2 inches (5.1 cm). Although wild silkworm moths are capable of flight, the domesticated moths kept in captivity no longer are. Humans carefully bred them so that the

insects lost this ability and are therefore more easily contained. Whether wild or domesticated, the adult moths live only for a few days, during which time they mate and the females lay eggs.

Making Silk

To make silk, industry producers collect the cocoons before the developing moth tears through them to emerge, and drop them into boiling water for a few minutes to dissolve a sticky substance the caterpillars also secreted while they were making their silken filaments. This gluey substance holds the cocoon together. Industry workers collect the unraveling silk and wind several of the fine fibers together to make one length of silk thread. This process kills the pupae, of course, but the silk workers save enough cocoons to ensure a thriving future population.

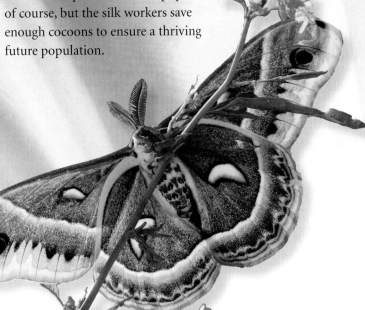

Below: A cecropia moth, a very large North American silkworm moth with boldly marked reddish brown wings.

Background: Luxurious silk fabric has been prized for millennia.

The Graveyard Shift

Although it is not a cemetery, a lot near a Tennessee medical center is filled with dead people. Some of the

Above: Blue bottle flies are some of the first insects to follow the scent of blood and gases to arrive on the body of a newly dead human or other animal. The female flies quickly begin laying eggs, which will hatch into maggots.

Right: In a homicide investigation, forensic scientists examine and collect insects, including the fly maggots shown here. Using their knowledge of insect behavior and development, the scientists can often accurately pinpoint the time of death.

bodies lie in plain sight, others planted barely below the ground or submerged in ponds. The site is called the University of Tennessee Forensic Anthropology Facility, and it has become a tool for teaching forensic entomology, more specifically the science of using insects to solve crimes.

Students regularly visit the facility and check each body for insect eggs, adult flies and beetles, maggots, and grubs. Through such

exercises as these, the students learn typical patterns of human decomposition, and use them to work backward and determine the time of death, an important piece of information in murder and other police investigations.

Macabre Insect Parade

Insects move in on a dead body on a remarkably regular schedule. One of the first to arrive is the bottle fly, a group of several fly species. Common members of this group are the blue bottle fly (*Calliphora vomitoria*) and the green bottle fly (*Phaenicia sericata*), which are similar to houseflies in appearance, although a bit larger, and with shiny blue or green bodies, respectively. These flies, also known as blowflies, home in on the smell of blood and of gases released by a newly deceased body and begin to feast on wounds, as well as the soft, moist tissue of the eyes, and inside

the nose and mouth. At these sites, the female flies will begin laying eggs that will soon hatch into maggots that will also feast on the corpse. Other flies and beetles also arrive at the lifeless body almost on cue, and many of these also lay eggs there.

Calendar of Death

When a forensic entomologist arrives at a crime scene, he or she checks the body for the types of insects present and their developmental stages. The entomologist typically preserves some of the eggs, maggots, and grubs at the exact developmental stage in which they were found, and also collects some living specimens to rear in the lab for precise determination of the species. The next step is to review the weather over the previous few days. Since insects are cold-blooded, warm or cold temperatures can speed or slow their development. By checking the developmental stages of the various insects and cross-referencing against daily ambient temperatures, the forensics expert can very precisely deduce the time of death.

Beyond Time

In some instances, insects can also reveal the place of death. Individual insect species prefer cooler to warmer temperatures, meadows to wetlands, or cityscapes to forests. When a

forensic entomologist finds a body in a location that does not match the insect decomposers on it, he or she may propose that the body was moved after death, another vital clue in crime scene investigations.

Deep-fried caterpillars are a common snack item in some parts of Asia.

MMMMMM . . . DRIED CATERPILLARS

Dried caterpillars are a good food source, according to the United Nations Food and Agriculture Organization (FAO). In a 2004 study, the organization touted the nutritional content of dried caterpillars, including a protein and fat content greater than a similar-sized portion of beef or fish. The study found that 70 percent of those surveyed in the Democratic Republic of Congo, 85 percent of those in the Central African Republic, and 91 percent of those in Botswana already ate the larval insects. An FAO press release announcing the study added: "Depending on the species, caterpillars are considered to be rich in minerals, such as potassium, calcium, magnesium, zinc, phosphorus, and iron, as well as various vitamins."

CHAPTER 11

INSECT COMMUNICATION

IN GENERAL, INSECTS ARE NOT VOCAL CREATURES. This does not mean that they do not communicate in other ways. Most people are familiar with the chirps of crickets and the screeching buzz of cicadas, but insect communication goes far beyond these two common summertime sounds.

As described earlier, ants, moths, and a great many other insects produce pheromones that provide maps to food. In certain instances, these pheromones may attract a male to a female, or vice versa, or may provide information about an impending threat, whether it be a predator or an insect-scale natural disaster. Beyond pheromones, communication avenues may include vibrations the insects make on plant leaves and stems. Researchers now believe such signals are a primary mode of conversation among leafhoppers and treehoppers and may be common among caterpillars, too. Another type of insect is known for the noises it makes by blowing air out of holes on the sides of its body. Some very common insect creatures have also made headlines over the years for their elaborate dances, the intricacies of which tell their nest mates exactly where to find a meal.

Left: Some ants excel in cooperation. Here, individuals link their bodies together to create a living bridge that others cross to carry food back to the nest. Inset: A small swarm of wasps is at work on its nest. The initial cells are round. It is when the wasps attach additional cells to the edges of existing ones that the cells begin to take on a hexagonal appearance.

Good Vibrations

This rhododendron leafhopper (*Graphocephala fennahi*) is striking in turquoise-green and scarlet. Scientists have recently become very interested in leafhoppers and treehoppers for the way they communicate: by making and listening to vibrations that are transmitted along the vegetation.

Sound is vibration. Humans hear vibrations transmitted through the air, but insects can hear vibrations transmitted through plants. Although we might not be able to detect their sounds, insects all around us are using these vibrations to communicate with one another.

Hoppers

Leafhoppers and treehoppers are the typically small insects that sit along the stems of plants or blades of grass, but will also bound into the air at a moment's notice. Easily overlooked as great communicators, these insects use their abdomens to make a vibrational racket in the vegetation.

By hooking up equipment to translate the insects' plant vibrations into human-audible sounds, scientists have revealed hoots followed by trembles, low-to-high swooping pitches, repeated *whoop-whoop-whoops*, various clicks, downward *aw-w-w* slides, and a plethora of other hopper noises.

What Are They Saying?

For the most part, hoppers call to find mates. A male makes his thumps, whistles, ticks, or moans, and an interested female responds with a typically much-less-elaborate drum during a silent part of the male's performance. Often, the drum results in a small stampede as every available male in the vicinity converges on the drummer.

Hoppers also communicate for other reasons, such as announcing an especially abundant food source or sounding an SOS. According to researcher Rex Cocroft of the University of Missouri, thorn bugs (*Umbonia crassicornis*) have an open line of communication between mother and offspring. Once a female lays her eggs, she stays with them until they hatch into nymphs and remains close for the next few weeks as they grow. During this period, if a nymph spots a predator, it will begin making short pulses. The other nymphs join in perfectly, and the synchronized cacophony beckons the mother, which arrives ready to kick out the attacker. If she is successful, she calms her brood with vibrations of her own.

Battle of the Vibrations

Besides leafhoppers and treehoppers, other insects rely on plant-borne vibrations to converse. One of them is the caterpillar of the arched hooktip (*Drepana arcuata*), a brown-striped, beige moth of North America. The caterpillar has a brown-and-green body that comes to a point at its posterior end. Perhaps its most unusual characteristic is its acoustical fights with other hooktip caterpillars. Researchers at Carleton University in Ottawa, Canada, and the University of Illinois studied the larvae either by allowing a caterpillar to make its "nest," which is a few strands of silk that partially curl a portion of leaf, or by placing the caterpillar on a leaf that already had a nest it could occupy. They then introduced a second caterpillar to the leaf. In repeated experiments, the original, or "resident" caterpillar fell back to the nest and commenced rapping and scraping the leaf with its mandibles and part of its abdomen. The interloper responded in kind. The resulting contests—all of which were recorded with microphones placed within 0.8 inch (2 cm) of the battle zone—lasted a few minutes to several hours, usually with the resident caterpillar coming out on top. Although this 2001 study was the first to show such territorial exchanges among caterpillars, the researchers believe it may be "a principal mode of communication of this important group of insects."

The caterpillar of the arched hooktip moth (*Drepana arcuata*) has the highly unusual habit of staging "acoustical" battles with rival hooktip caterpillars.

IS THAT A JET?

Like clockwork, every 17 years in the eastern United States an odd-looking insect arises from the ground by the hundreds of thousands and begins to sing—loudly. These are the 17-year cicadas (*Magicicada septendecim*), insects with red eyes, long wings, and wide bodies about 1.5 inches (3.8 cm) long. Their song is actually a mating call produced when a male vibrates a drumlike membrane, or tymbal, on its abdomen to produce a racket sometimes compared with a fire alarm or jetliner taking off. From an inch (2.5 cm) away, the sound measures 100 decibels, the same loudness as a chain saw. According to the National Institute on Deafness and Other Communication Disorders, just 85 decibels are enough to damage a person's ears. Fortunately, the din is short-lived. Their mating season lasts about six weeks, and afterward they disappear from our view for another 17 years.

The northern United States is home to three species of periodical cicadas, all in the genus *Magicicada*. Within each species, including this *Magicicada septendecim*, its members emerge en masse from the ground every 17 years to mate. Besides their sheer numbers, the males make their presence known with their earsplitting mating calls.

Hissing Cockroaches

The Madagascan giant hissing cockroach (*Gromphadorhina portentosa*) pictured here can reach 3 inches (7.6 cm) long, but it is not the world's largest cockroach. At a whopping 8.4 inches (3.3 cm) in length, the giant rhinoceros cockroach (*Macropanesthia rhinoceros*) of Australia holds that title.

The large, whitish wings on this young adult American cockroach (*Periplaneta americana*) lie flat atop and conceal its abdomen from view. As it ages, the wings will likely darken. It usually gets around by running, but it can also glide with its wings held taut, and can engage in flapping flight.

In almost any live-insect exhibit, one of the stars of the show is the hissing cockroach (*Gromphadorhina portentosa*). They are some of the largest cockroaches in the world, but it is not only their size that reels in an audience. It is also their sound.

Basic Body Plan

The hissing cockroach is one of 4,000 cockroach species living in the world today. All, including those sometimes called water bugs, are members of the same order, called Blattodea. The average cockroach has an oval-shaped, flattened body and a large, shieldlike pronotum that completely or nearly hides the head when viewing the cockroach from above. Two long antennae, however, are clearly visible. It typically holds its six long legs in a widely straddled position, and gets them moving very quickly when trying to avoid a predator. The average cockroach is brown, black, or a combination of both, sometimes with a lime-green hue or a reddish cast, but immediately after they molt, they may be white to tan for a short time until the tanning of the exoskeleton is complete.

The smallest members of the cockroach order are the Wheeler ant cockroaches (*Attaphila fungicola*), which measure only 0.1 to 0.2 inches (3–4 mm) long. Their name comes from their out-of-the-ordinary living arrangements, located inside the nests of leafcutter ants. The hissing cockroach typically reaches 2 to 3 inches (5.1–7.6 cm) in length, but the title of world's largest usually goes to the giant rhinoceros cockroach (*Macropanesthia rhinoceros*), also known as the giant burrowing cockroach. This insect, which lives underground in Australia, can reach 3.3 inches (8.4 cm) in length. Both the hissing cockroach and the giant rhinoceros cockroach are wingless, but many other species of cockroaches have large, membranous wings and are capable of flight. Wings or not, though, cockroaches usually stick to the ground and get around by walking and running. The winged species hold their wings, which are longer than the body, flat on top of the abdomen.

The Hiss

The hissing cockroach is unusual for the audible hisses it makes. Like other insects, the cockroach takes in

and expels oxygen through the small openings, or spiracles, along its abdomen rather than through nostrils as many other animals do. The hissing cockroach makes its *whoosh* sound by forcing air out of two of its spiracles. To an untrained human ear, a hiss is just a hiss, but to other cockroaches and the researchers who study them, the sounds come in four varieties, three of them made only by males.

Males will hiss one way to court a potential female mating partner; another to defend its territory, which may harbor several females, from other male cockroaches; and a third way as a battle cry, used when a second male disregards the territorial hiss and tries to move in on the harem. Ensuing fights are usually short-lived, with one pushing the other away. Visitors to a living-insect exhibit can often hear the fourth variety of hiss emanating from any cockroach, male or female. The creatures make this hiss when they feel bothered, which frequently occurs when an exhibitor picks up one of the cockroaches to show the crowd.

This hissing cockroach makes its sound by forcing air out through two of the holes that run along the sides of its abdomen. The holes, called spiracles, are the openings through which cockroaches (and other insects) breathe.

Summer Orchestra

Above: Crickets, such as these field crickets (*Gryllus bimaculatus*), communicate with chirps. The males are the noisemakers and produce the sound by pulling a "file" on one wing across a "scraper" on the other.

Below right: According to legend, the katydid's name comes from its chirps. In some species, the chirp pattern resembles the syllable count and timing in the phrase "Katy-did, katy-didn't." The leaflike katydid pictured here hails from Ecuador.

If cockroaches are the wind instruments of an insect orchestra and leafhoppers handle the percussion, then the string section would have to be the grasshoppers, katydids, and crickets. All of these insects produce their sounds by pulling one body part over another, rather like a violinist draws a bow across a violin's strings.

Crickets

Chirping among crickets is a male thing. He makes the sound by raising his front wings and sliding one across the other. In the field cricket (*Gryllus bimaculatus*), for example, one vein on each of the front wings has small teeth on it. This is known as the file. The outer edge of each wing, called the scraper, is hard and sharp. By pulling the file on one wing along the scraper of the other, a process called stridulation, he produces the chirp. According to research at the Universities of Leicester and Nottingham in the United Kingdom, the vibration of the wings and the air space under the wings fine-tunes and amplifies the chirp.

Female crickets and people who take the time to listen to male cricket calls can tell the chirps of one species of cricket from the next. A female will respond only to a male of her own species, and only when he is making his mating call. Males also typically produce territorial calls and sometimes alarm calls. Both male and female crickets can hear. They perceive sound in the same general way that humans do, but their "ear drums," or tympana, are on the front legs rather than inside the head.

Katydids

The call of the katydid is another familiar warm-weather sound. As with the crickets, the males are the primary callers, but the females in some katydid species will respond to males with chirps of their own. Katydids are also similar to crickets in the location of their hearing drums, and in the way they stridulate. Their wings are likewise set up with the file and scraper, and they draw the file across the scraper. According to insect lore, their collective name comes from the call of several species, which has a rhythm of *katy-did, katy-didn't.*

Grasshoppers

Grasshoppers stridulate, too, but they do it differently. A grasshopper rubs the insides of its hind legs (the area comparable to our thighs) either against its abdomen or against its forewings to make its scraping noise. Again, the males are the main communicators, generally with territory and courtship calls, and in many cases a separate call during or after mating. As well as these calls, both male and female adults make another sound, but it has more to do with locomotion than communication. When they leap into flight, the rapid flapping of their hind wings generates a snapping noise. Although a few grasshopper species have no tympana, most

Typically grass green, this snowy tree cricket (*Oecanthus fultoni*) appears a bit browner in color as it sits on a yellow prairie flower. It is also known as a thermometer cricket, because the male's regular chirps can be used to determine the temperature.

CRICKET METEOROLOGIST

Want the temperature? Throw out your thermometer and listen to a snowy tree cricket (*Oecanthus fultoni*). This odd-looking cricket with its long green body and red antennae announces the temperature with its monotonous, regularly spaced chirps. Cold-blooded, as are all insects, its body temperature fluctuates with the ambient temperature. This, in turn, slows down or speeds up its call. To determine the outdoor temperature in Fahrenheit, simply count the number of chirps in 13 seconds and add 40. This formula works for crickets living in the eastern United States. The snowy tree crickets living in the western United States chirp a little differently, so the temperature works out to the number of chirps in 12.5 seconds plus 38. When using either formula, remember that the number it yields represents the temperature at the location of the cricket. You may be standing someplace a few degrees warmer or cooler.

do. Unlike the crickets and katydids, their drums are located on either side of the first segment of the abdomen, just behind the thorax.

Interpretive Dance

Just as people often try out restaurants based on the advice of friends or family members, honey bees will fly off to a new food source on the recommendation of a fellow forager. Cartoons may show a forager leading a flying swarm to a flowery shrub, but the actual communication method bees use is far more interesting.

This computer illustration of dancing honey bees (*Apis mellifera*) shows how a foraging bee (center) tells the surrounding bees about the location of food it has found. After returning to the hive, the foraging bee squirms in a figure-eight pattern that reveals the position of the food and its distance.

Round Dance

The round dance is the simpler of the two interpretive dances honey bees use to tell one another about a good dining spot. When a forager finds food nearby, it collects some nectar and pollen and flies back inside the dark hive to tell the others. It begins wiggling and walking in a circle, turns around, and retraces

the circle backward. It continues in this repeated round dance while other foragers crowd around, picking up the smell of the food source from the dancer. They then fly off, fanning out from the hive to search for the matching scent. This works well for food in the immediate area, but another dance is necessary for more distant treasures.

Waggle Dance

For nectar that is more than about 160 feet (49 m) away—a little more for some hives and less for others—the forager must not only convey the type of food through the scent of nectar and pollen on its body, but also tell the other bees where to find it. In 1949, Austrian-born zoologist Karl von Frisch suggested that the bees use a waggle dance to communicate very precisely the food's direction and distance from the hive.

In this dance, the forager wiggles its abdomen while strutting out a pattern on one of the vertical combs inside the nest. The forager walks a straight line, then veers up and around, or down and around to go back to the beginning of the straight line, and begins again. The result is a wide figure-eight. If the direction of the food is toward the sun, the dancer keeps the straight portion of the pattern completely vertical on the comb. If it is off to the right of the sun by 5 degrees, the forager tilts the straight line 5 degrees to the right. By adjusting the angle of the straight portion of the dance in this manner, the forager can exactly convey the food's direction.

For the distance, the dancer shortens or lengthens the straight run and changes the frequency of its abdomen wiggles during the performance. As they do with the round dance, the other bees crowd around the dancer, this time paying close attention to its movements with their antennae while picking up the scent of the nectar and pollen.

In 1949, Karl von Frisch (1886–1982) first described how bees use a dance to convey the precise location of food. In 1973, he shared the Nobel Prize for Physiology or Medicine with Konrad Lorenz and Nikolaas Tinbergen "for their discoveries concerning organization and elicitation of individual and social behavior patterns."

A Current View

Since Frisch's work, many scientists have studied the use of dance in insect communication. A recent example is a 2005 study that used radar to track the flight paths of individual honey bees and found that the insects can indeed follow the instructions provided in a forager's waggle dance. The study, conducted by researchers at Rothamsted Research and University of Greenwich in the United Kingdom, and the Institute for Biology in Berlin, showed that most of the bees recruited by a dancer "almost immediately undertook a straight flight of direction and length that brought them directly into the vicinity" of the food source.

THE BEAT GOES ON

The irritating buzz of a mosquito or fly and the attention-grabbing whir as a wasp flies past are sounds produced by the flapping of their wings. Those that flap the fastest have the highest-pitched buzz. A typical blowfly beats its wings at a rate of 200 flaps per second, while a mosquito clocks in a bit faster at 300 to 600, and therefore has a higher pitch. The fastest-known wing beat among the insects, and indeed among any animal species, is that of the biting midge in the genus *Forcipomyia*. It flaps at the astonishing rate of 1,046 beats per second.

The elm sawfly, or *Cimbex americana*.

CHAPTER 12

SIX-LEGGED SOCIETY

OTHER THAN MATING AND PERHAPS STAYING with their offspring for a short time, most insects spend their time on Earth alone. A few of these otherwise-solitary insects spice things up with gregarious periods, such as the mass butterfly migrations or the occasional feeding swarms among the grasshoppers and locusts. Fully social insects, on the other hand, do more than share the same location. Fully social, or eusocial, insects live and work together with other members of their species, dividing up into several labor categories, or castes, to handle different chores, such as gathering food, feeding and caring for the young, defending the communal nest, and reproducing. Examples are ants, bees, and termites, as well as earwigs.

In addition, a number of insects form relationships with other species. The arrangement between insect pollinators and plants is mutually beneficial, as is the association described below in which one insect provides bodyguard services in exchange for food from the protected species. Relationships are not always so well-balanced. In some cases, one species may receive a positive effect as the result of an association, while another reaps no reward or gets the short end of the stick.

Left: The members of this bee colony swarm over their hive. Like other fully social insects, they split up the work so that different individuals are responsible for finding food, taking part in reproduction, and caring for the young. Inset: Although most insects are mainly solitary individuals, ants live in societies. Here, a colony of ants works together to tend its anthill.

Termites

Right: In North America, most termites build their nests underground, although some wood-eating varieties can cause considerable damage to buildings. Termites in other areas of the world, especially the tropics, build large, visible structures called mounds, or termitaria. This termite mound is located in the Shaba Game Reserve, Kenya.

Below: Like other termite species, members of a colony of Formosan subterranean termites belong to different castes with separate jobs. A colony's queen, such as the one pictured here, has a baglike, egg-containing abdomen, which becomes larger and more productive as she ages.

Center: Although they are native to East Asia, Formosan subterranean termites (*Coptotermes formosanus*) have made a second home for themselves in the southern United States. In 1998, the U.S. government instituted Operation Full Stop, a program to fight the insects, which cause considerable damage to buildings. Shown here is a soldier, identifiable by its dark, oval head and powerful jaws.

Termites are social insects, many of which also have a mutually beneficial relationship with other organisms, namely bacteria. The connection to the bacteria is a critical association for these termites, because they eat wood but do not have the enzyme necessary to digest it. The bacteria do. Without the enzyme, a termite can eat wood nonstop and still die of starvation. Fortunately for the insect, the bacteria exist quite well inside the termite's digestive tract, and use the enzyme, which is called cellulase, to break down the wood, thereby providing nutrition for themselves and for the termites.

Castes

A typical termite colony has the following members:

- a king and a queen, which handle all of the reproductive tasks;
- several nymphs that have the potential to take over the job of king or queen should the need arise;
- soldiers, which are large-jawed individuals that defend the nest;
- and workers, which perform all other tasks from building the nest to foraging for food and caring for the king and queen's offspring.

Life Cycle

A colony has its start when new, young kings and queens fly away from the nests of their parents. As they land on vegetation, both the male and female lose their wings, and they crawl away together to set up housekeeping, perhaps in a fallen log or rotting tree trunk. The queen's abdomen grows with the eggs inside and soon takes on the appearance of a giant maggot hundreds—and sometimes thousands—of times larger than the worker termites and her mate. Her job and the king's is to continue producing offspring, and they are good at it. The queen in some species lays 20,000 to 30,000 eggs per day.

During the lifetime of the king and queen, which may span a decade, the termite nest continues to expand. Certain termites,

including most of those in the United States, build their nests as a series of underground tunnels. Other species, especially those in the tropics, build huge mounding structures, called termitaria, that may reach 10 feet (3 m) tall or higher.

Along with the king and queen, termites have worker and soldier castes. The workers are wingless and have the general look of an ant, but their wider waists give them away. The soldier termites are easily distinguishable from the workers because the soldiers have enormous jaws that are excellent for fighting off predators. The large mouthparts in the soldiers of many species are not, however, efficient for eating termite food, so the workers must feed the soldiers.

Nasty but Necessary

Wood-eating termites periodically lose their gut flora and replace it in a way that people usually find revolting. During molting, when the termite sloughs its old "skin," it also loses the lining of its digestive system, which contains the bacteria. To get them back, the insect gobbles down other termites' feces, which contain still-living bacteria and protozoa. One family of termites, the Termitidae, apparently bypasses bacteria and protozoa and instead uses fungus to aid its digestion.

SPECIFICATIONS

Insects: Termites
Order: Isoptera
Meaning of Isoptera: "like wings," referring to the similar size and appearance of all wings in reproductive adults
Typical characteristics of adults in this order:
- antlike, but with a wider waist
- straight antennae that resemble a string of pearls in structure
- among the reproductive adults, two pair of similarly sized, long membranous wings that drop off following mating
- larvae are called nymphs and look much like wingless adults

DIVERSITY
Number of known species: 1,900–2,300
Size: Most adults are in the range of 0.1 to 0.6 inches (0.25–1.5 cm) in length, but the queens may be much larger. In the yellow-necked termite (*Kalotermes flavicollis*) of Europe and the Middle East, for example, the queen at 0.6 inches (1.5 cm) is about twice as long as the worker termites. The queen of the African species *Macrotermes bellicosus* may hold the title of the longest termite. She can grow to 5.5 inches (14 cm) long.
Sampling of benefits to humans: People eat termites, especially the large queens, which are considered a delicacy in some cultures. Other animals also dine on termites. Termites, in turn, eat wood and aid the decomposition process that ultimately creates richer soil.

Some termites build mounded nests. These mounds, constructed by magnetic termites (*Amitermes meridionalis*), dot the landscape of Australia's Northern Territory. The termites' name comes from their propensity to build their fingerlike mounds in a north-south orientation. The mounds may be as tall as 13.1 feet (4 m).

Honey Bees

Right: Unlike a termite queen that looks little like her nestmates, a queen honey bee is only slightly different. The queen, at the center, has a larger thorax and abdomen than the workers surrounding her on the hive.

Background: Honey-filled comb, ready for harvest.

Honey bees have social hierarchies similar to but not the same as the termites'. One of the major differences is that most of the honey bees are female.

Girls Rule

For the vast majority of animals, an offspring develops only from a fertilized egg. An egg becomes fertilized when the chromosomes it contains are combined with the chromosomes from a male's sperm cell, and the fertilized egg has even odds of becoming a male or a female. Social bees, ants, and wasps turn this whole scheme on its head. In their world, all of the fertilized eggs—those with a mix of chromosomes from the mother's, or queen's, egg and the father's sperm—become females. In addition, the queen can stop the sperm from reaching some of her eggs. This would be the end of the line for typical animal eggs, but unfertilized ant, bee, and wasp eggs

develop without a hitch into males. In other words, the sex of the offspring is not left to chance in these social insects, but is instead determined by the queen. Scientists describe this system as "haplodiploid" to reflect the single (*haplo-*) or double (*di-*) contingent of chromosomes in the developing egg.

In such haplodiploid societies, a female worker devotes herself to the hive. Female honey bees will even go so far as to die for the colony by stinging a perceived predator. What does she get for the effort? Her genes live on. Although the worker does not have children of her own, she does have plenty of sisters, who share an average of 75 percent of her genes. Think of it this way: the genetic makeup that drives the worker's selfless behavior is echoed in the colony's next generations—her younger sisters who will have likewise altruistic characteristics.

"The little bee returns with evening's gloom/To join her comrades in the braided hive/Where . . . they dream their polity shall long survive."

—CHARLES TENNYSON TURNER

A Bee's Life

A honey bee's life begins as an egg laid by a queen into one of the slots in the honeycomb. When it hatches into a larva in about three days, worker bees begin arriving with food. For most female larvae, the workers start them off with salivary secretions, called royal jelly, and then switch to a pollen-and-honey mix called beebread. All of these female larvae will eventually develop into worker bees. Sometimes, however, the workers feed a larva nothing but royal jelly. These females develop into queens. For the honey bee, then, ascent to the throne is not a matter of breeding but one of feeding.

The larvae all pupate before emerging as adults, and then take on their grownup chores. The newest adults help with the care of the eggs and larvae, but soon graduate to building the comb and guarding it, and finally step up to the job of foraging for food.

A New Hive

Usually, the queen monitors the honeycomb for developing queen larvae and kills them. Occasionally, however, she allows one or more to live and sets off with a large swarm of the hive's workers to start over in a new hive. The remaining, new queen begins her reign in the old hive by flying into the air to mate with one or more of the males, which are called drones. This is her only mating for the year. She stores the sperm inside her body and doles it out to her eggs over the next year. After the mating flight, the drones' job is completed and they contribute nothing else to the hive. Their lack of usefulness does not get by the workers, which either chase them off or kill them and toss their bodies from the hive.

A honey bee queen lays one egg at a time, each inside its own wax cell in the hive. Here, two of the eggs have hatched into larvae.

Although the United States has a large population of honey bees, including many housed in hive boxes, honey bees are actually an introduced species in North America.

FOREIGN BEES

Honey bees have been in the Americas for so long, it is easy to forget that they are an introduced species native to Europe, Asia, and Africa. The first hives arrived with the European colonists, who brought them to New World shores in the 1600s. Some of the bees promptly escaped to the wild, and now North America has both captive, cultivated honey bees and wild populations.

Not Quite Society Types

Webspinners produce silken threads that they make into webs and tunnels. This webspinner, known only by its scientific name of *Clothoda urichi*, sits on its web. A female of this species will cover her eggs with silk, along with chewed bark and her own feces, until the eggs are ready to hatch.

Insect adults in general are not what would be described as "doting parents." Many simply lay their eggs and leave their offspring to fend for themselves. At the other end of the spectrum, the fully social insects have entire systems in place to provide round-the-clock nanny, maid, and chef services for growing larvae in the nest. Between these two extremes fall the so-called subsocial insects that live together at least temporarily in small, usually family groups and exhibit some type of brood care, such as feeding the young or protecting them from potential predators.

Webspinners

Webspinners are tiny insects 0.6 inches (1.5 cm) long or smaller that produce silk with glands uniquely located in their front legs. With back-and-forth swings of their forelegs, the insects look almost as if they are knitting the silk, and in a way, they are. By working in a small group, the webspinners create a connecting maze of silken tunnels under leaves, peeling bark, and stones.

Female webspinners and their offspring, which have no wings, remain mainly within the silken maze, where they scurry forward and backward through its tunnels. As the male nymphs become adults, they develop two pairs of long, slender wings. When they head forward through the tunnels, the wings lie flat against the abdomen, but when they run backward, the wings conveniently flip over to point in the opposite direction. The adult males do not eat at all, but before starving to death they usually have enough time to fly off in search of a landbound mate and start a new webspinner colony.

Burying Beetles

Its habit of burying dead animals as big as a mouse or a sparrow makes the American burying beetle (*Nicrophorus americanus*) one bizarre creature. The habit also makes the adult male and female beetles attentive parents.

Insects: Earwigs
Order: Dermaptera
Meaning of Dermaptera: "skin wing," referring to the short, tough forewings
Typical characteristics of adults in this order:
- slender body that ends in a pair of pincerlike structures, the cerci, also known as forceps
- long antennae that may be more than half as long as the body
- if present, a large pair of membranous hind wings that are folded up and stowed away under short, leathery forewings, called tegmina
- biting mouthparts
- the larvae are called nymphs and look much like the adults

DIVERSITY
Number of known species: 1,200–1,900
Size: Earwigs in the genus *Forficulina* are some of the smallest members of the order, growing to just 0.2 inches (4 mm) long from the head to the tip of the cerci as adults. The St. Helena earwig (*Labidura herculeana*), at 2.8 to 3.1 inches (7–8 cm) long, is the largest known earwig. Scientists fear that this earwig, which has only been found on St. Helena Island off the western coast of Africa, may now be extinct.
Sampling of benefits to humans: Earwigs often feed on rotting fruit and vegetables, and other decaying plant matter, and therefore participate in the recycling of nutrients to the ecosystem.

When the glossy black, orange-flecked beetles detect the smell of death, they race to the newly deceased corpse and start burying it. Because the insects are only about 1.5 inches (3.8 cm) in length, the chore may seem beyond their capabilities, but they have a rock-solid technique. They find the nearest area of soft, easy-digging soil, and then trot back to the corpse, flip upside down, and scoot underneath it. From this position, they use their legs to lift and pass the body forward much as college students hoist a cheerleader above their heads and pass her down a bleacher row. Once the corpse is properly located, the beetles set it down and start digging dirt from underneath the body while tossing dirt on top. In one night the beetles can complete the entire burial.

Their work does not end there. The beetles continue with the body preparations by removing its feathers or fur, pushing the leftover flesh into a ball, and slathering the ball with saliva. The female lays her eggs above the mass. As they hatch into larvae, the mother and father regurgitate food for their larvae to eat. Soon, the larvae begin feeding themselves from the corpse, and when all but the bones of the carcass is devoured, the larvae pupate and the adults finally leave.

Truly bizarre insects, burying beetles (genus *Nicrophorus*) turn recently deceased mammals and birds into nurseries for their eggs and eventually food sources for their hatching larvae. Their name comes from their practice of digging the dead animal into the ground.

This European earwig (*Forficula auricularia*) may look harmless, but humans have long feared them. According to one old wives' tale, earwigs will crawl into human ears while their victim is sleeping and burrow into the brain.

NOT-SO-SCARY EARWIGS

Despite the many, gory campfire tales and occasional science-fiction movie scenes about these insects crawling into a person's ear and burrowing into the brain, earwigs have no interest in entering any orifice, auditory or otherwise, on a human's body. The common earwig (*Forficula auricularia*), for instance, typically lives in family units under a rock or log, or in the dark corner of a basement.

Cross-species Relationships

Win-win situations are rare enough among humans that such successful relationships often get headlines. Cross-species insect associations can be just as difficult. Some result in mutually beneficial relationships, but others have clear winners and losers.

Ants and Aphids

Some of the most well-known mutualisms are between ants and aphids. Aphids live in colonies so thick that they can coat expanses of plant stems and leaves. The tiny insects drink great quantities of plant juices. The plant juices contain only small quantities of proteins, but high levels of sugars, therefore the insects ingest excess sugars while getting the proteins they need. As a result, their bodies excrete drops of

In an amazing cross-species lifestyle, certain species of ants and much smaller aphids have a mutually beneficial relationship. The ants provide protection for the vulnerable aphids, and the aphids secrete sweet fluid called honeydew that feeds the ants.

sweet fluid, called honeydew, as a waste product. Ants, including species in the genera *Tapinoma*, cherish the honeydew and act as protecting shepherds for herds of aphids. Both sides come out on top: the aphids receive security in exchange for the food they provide to their bodyguards.

Fly versus Fly versus Human

In the tropics of North, Central, and South America, a human invader lurks. It is the torsalo (*Dermatobia hominis*), also known as a human bot fly or warble fly, the maggots of which burrow under a person's skin. They then live there for one and a half to two and a half months before coming to the surface to fall off and pupate. Since the adult torsalo is a loud, buzzing insect about 0.6 inches (1.5 cm) in length, it might seem that a person should be

WELCOME, SPECIAL GERMS!

If all of the TV ads promoting antibacterial cleaning products are any indication, Americans are fixated on eliminating all bacteria from their homes. Some insects, conversely, are inviting certain ones in. One is a black-and-yellow, solitary wasp called a beewolf (*Philanthus triangulum*), which gets its name from the female's practice of hunting down honey bees to feed her young. The female is also unusual because she oozes drops of a bacteria-filled substance from glands on her antennae and lays her eggs next to them, according to researchers at Germany's University of Würzburg. Their 2005 study suggests that the bacteria in the substance help the growing larvae fight off disease from fungi.

able to swat it or shoo it away before it can lay its eggs. This would be true if the adult actually laid its eggs on its human host, but it does not. The female fly takes hold of a smaller fly species, such as a mosquito, and sticks its eggs to the captive's body. The captive flies off, unharmed and unhampered by the added weight of the eggs, and carries on its daily business. When it lands on a person or other warm-blooded animal, the larvae in the eggs sense the body heat, quickly hatch, and start burrowing. In humans, a buried maggot typically results in a raised red bump and, depending on its location, varying degrees of pain. In this unusual three-way association, the torsalo is the only participant that comes out ahead. The egg carrier is largely unaffected and the person or other animal that serves as the maggot's nursery incurs a significant risk of infection.

Slavemaker Ants

It may seem simple to determine whether a particular species benefits from a relationship with another organism, but the association between slavemaker ants and their slaves (usually members of other ant species) leaves scientists scratching their heads. For years, researchers assumed that the slaves, the smaller of the two species, were clearly getting a raw deal. After all, the slavemaker ants were raiding their colony, absconding with larvae and pupae, and as the young grew, forcing them to work in the captor's nest. Recent research at the Universities of Manitoba and Toronto, however, suggests that slavemakers in the species *Protomognathus americanus* actually treat their slaves well, and even tend to any of the developing queen larvae they may have captured so that they can fly off to start new colonies.

Most members of the genus *Philanthus* prey on bees, a behavior that gives them their common names of beewolves. This black-and-yellow beewolf, *Philanthus triangulum*, started life as did other beewolves: by devouring an invertebrate prey delivered by its mother.

LIFE CYCLE **PART 4**

CHAPTER 13

COURTING BEHAVIOR

A BOX OF CHOCOLATES AND A ROSE, a dab of cologne, soft music, perhaps a night of dancing and a flashy suit—these are all common ways that men woo women. Male insects use similar lures to attract females. Although they may not offer candy and flowers, some male insects do present the females with gifts of food, sometimes in well-wrapped packages. Many males (and some females) attract potential mates with "colognes" of pheromones that may waft through the air for long distances before tantalizing a member of the opposite sex. In lieu of popping in a CD, many insects opt for their own "mood" music. Their serenades, however, may not emanate from the mouth, but from a separate area of the body—including the reproductive structure itself. Some insects forgo audible sounds and rely instead on vibrations of a different sort. For example, a number of aquatic species create ripples in the water surface to draw potentially interested partners. A variety of insects also participate in courtship "dances," ritualized movements that set the stage for mating. The flashiest dancers among the insects include those males with vibrant colors and, not surprisingly, those species that literally flash.

Left: A firefly (family Lampyridae) flashes its abdomen while climbing a plant stem. More than mere decoration, the flashes are the small beetle's means of communication. Inset: Members of the Arctiidae family of moths, such as this cream-spot tiger (*Arctia villica*), reach out to other members of their species by making ultrasonic sounds with a special organ on the thorax. Humans may not be able to hear them, but moths—and some other animals—can. Pages 140–141: The familiar ladybug beetle is well known for its hibernation patterns.

Alluring Aromas

For the moths, which are mainly nocturnal creatures, visual displays are not of much use in attracting a mating partner from more than a few feet (about a meter) away. Odors, however, can reel in the opposite sex day or night.

The male ceanothus moth (*Hyalophora euryalus*) has enormous, feathery antennae to pick up the scent signal, called a pheromone, of a female.

The Signal

Female silkworms (*Bombyx mori*) are known for more than producing silk. When they metamorphose into adult moths, they also release a pheromone that acts as a powerful advertisement of their availability for mating.

Knowledge of the pheromone's alluring chemical molecule came from work done by an extraordinarily dogged German scientist, Adolf Butenandt (1903–95), in the 1930s through the 1950s. Butenandt and his research group meticulously snipped off the pheromone-producing glands at the tips of the abdomens of about a half million female silkworm moths. They crushed the tips, separated the pheromone into its component chemical compounds, and tested their male-drawing power. Butenandt announced his findings in 1959, and named the compound bombykol after the moth's genus name.

The Response

Each moth species has its own identifying pheromone. In the typical wild moth, the female releases the pheromone, and males, sometimes from distances of several miles, will follow the scent toward her. Humans have bred the domesticated male silkworm moths so that they cannot fly, but the males still register their response to bombykol by rapidly flapping their wings. Wild male moths, on the other hand, usually fly a crooked line to the female, veering one way to the other to

pick up the pheromone and sometimes doubling back if they have lost the trail. As they approach, some males may release a pheromone of their own. This odor is not to help the female find him, but to put her in the mood for mating.

Male moths detect the female's pheromone with highly attuned antennae. In many species, including the silkworm moth, the male's antennae are feathery plumes that are equipped with numerous sensors to pick up only the female's phero-mone. According to 2003 research at the University of Cagliari in Italy and the Swedish University of Agricultural Sciences, moth antennae are able to detect minute quantities of pheromones as well as plant aromas. The researchers outfitted male and female Egyptian cotton leaf worm moths (*Spodoptera littoralis*) with electrodes to monitor heart activity. The scientists released just either 5 molecules of the pheromone or about 10 molecules of the plant odor during a one-second interval. The moths appeared outwardly to

not notice the odors, but the electrodes revealed an increased heart rate that indicated that they were fully aware of the scents in the air. The researchers concluded that the moth's odor-detection system was more sensitive than "anything earlier reported in any organism."

Other Scented Insects

Moths are only one of many insects that use pheromones to entice a mate. Some butterflies, such as the male monarch (*Danaus plexippus*), produce the odor through scent glands on their wings. These glands are clearly vis-ible as black blotches approximately in the middle of each hind wing. Other insects, including beetles, also use pheromones to attract the opposite sex. The scents are so effective that the pheromones and phero-monelike substances have been added to commercial products designed for trapping pest species.

Above: Unlike many butter-flies and moths, in which the female produces the pheromone for the male to follow, female monarch butterflies (*Danaus plexippus*) follow the scent of the males. The system appears to have worked well for this mating pair of monarchs.

Below: The male monarch produces its pheromones with two scent glands. Each gland is visible in the photo as a dark blotch on a vein at approximately the center of the hind wings.

All the Right Moves

Above: In the fall, huge swarms of monarch butterflies migrate from colder climates to warmer ones. At their wintering grounds, millions may roost together. Before they start their return migration the following spring, they mate.

Right: Tiny at 0.35 inches (9 mm) long, this male dance fly (*Empis livida*) and other males in the family Empididae put females in the mood for mating by performing something akin to a line dance. The males gather in the air to form a dense cloud and rise and fall in a mass movement. Females then swoop into the cloud to mate.

Most daytime-active insects rely not on pheromones to seal the mating deal, but on ritual movements, called dances. Some, such as the monarch butterflies and the closely related queen butterfly (*Danaus gilippus*), use both methods to secure a mate.

Butterfly Choreography

The typical courtship dance of monarchs and queen butterflies has several steps that culminate with copulation. Once a female gets nears a male, the choreography begins. The male chases the female in flight, and at the same time extends a burst of pheromone-doused, hairlike appendages, called hair pencils, from the end of his abdomen. He then flies just over the female and lowers to brush the hair pencils against her head and antennae. She responds by landing, and he continues to hover over her and to titillate her with his hair pencils. When she finally folds her wings up over her body, he lands alongside and they mate, often taking off again while still attached at the abdomen— he above and she dangling below upside down.

Dance Flies

People generally encounter dance flies (in the family Empididae) when out for a lake- or streamside stroll on an early-summer evening. Dance flies are the gnat-sized insects that occasionally swarm around a person's head and make even the least physically fit individual take up at least a little jogging to get away from them. In many species of the flies, the thick cloud of insects is made solely of males that move as a coherent unit, flying several feet higher into the air and then dropping back down. The repeated rise and fall of the swarm is for the benefit of females, which are watching the display from nearby vegetation. When the females are excited enough, they fly in groups into the male swarm. Each male attempts to clutch a passing female, and when one of them is successful, the pair of dance flies drops from the swarm to the ground, where they mate.

Laboratory fruit flies (*Drosophila melanogaster*), shown here clustered on a piece of glass, combine dancing with pheromones during their courtship. These small insects are common subjects of experiments and have led to a greater understanding of genetics.

Fruit Flies

The ubiquitous laboratory fruit fly (*Drosophila melanogaster*) also has a ritualized "dance" that occurs hand-in-hand with female pheromones. The male begins his pattern of courtship movements, including touching his front legs to the female. The front legs contain receptors that perceive the female's pheromones. Once he senses the pheromones, the male continues with a wing-vibrating routine and finally runs his mouthparts—specifically, the end of his upper and lower "lips" (the labium and labrum)—over her before mating. Because he uses his mouthparts to pick up surface odors rather than his antennae to detect airborne scents, the fruit fly tastes rather than smells the pheromone. According to research at Duke University, the pheromone is a key step in the dance. A male fly that was missing the pheromone receptors on its forelegs could not detect the female's odor encouragement and would cut the dance short. For successful mating in this species, the male's green light for mating is the female's pheromone, and the female's go-ahead signal is the male's dance.

Wedding Presents

For many male insects, a longer mating act is better. Quick copulation typically means that few of the male's sperm have had time to transfer to the female's reproductive tract, and therefore have no chance to ultimately result in offspring. One way that the male of some species ensures a long sexual encounter is by giving the female a nuptial gift, usually a little meal to keep her busy while he takes care of his business.

Wrap It Up

Many male dance flies do more than put on a nice air show to entice females. They also come bearing gifts. For these predaceous insects, the gift is often a dead insect, such as a midge, that the dance fly was able to impale with its

Dance flies, including the species *Empis tesselata* pictured here, use their long, beaklike snouts to stab insect prey. Males of many species hang on to the dead insects and use them as gifts to lure potential mates.

piercing beak of a mouth. The males bring their prizes to the swarm, and the females fly in to find a mate. The males with the biggest gifts stand out from the crowd. In some species of dance flies, the pattern is a little different. The females are the ones that swarm while the males look for appropriate prey items. A gift-holding male then flitters into a roiling cloud of females, presents his gift to one of them, and if she accepts, the mating begins. The longer it takes her to eat the meal, the longer he has to mate, and therefore, more of his sperm are transferred.

Some male dance flies try a different tack that prolongs the mating period further. They envelop their gift in silk (that they secrete), forcing the female to take the time to unwrap it. In some species, the male dance flies are more devious. Rather than wrap a gift in silk, they present the female with only a wad of silk. By the time she unwraps it and realizes it is empty, he has already mated with her.

Not Exactly Chocolates

Some gift-giving males stray from insect prey and give the females something more personal. The fire-colored beetles (*Neopyrochroa flabellata*) are an example. These black and orange insects have a pair of saw-toothed antennae that provide considerable

1996 research at Cornell University. If she is pleased with the secretion, she allows the male to mate with her. During the process, he releases much of his remaining cantharidin with his sperm. The chemical then disperses over her eggs and provides a protective effect against predators, which avoid cantharidin-laced foods.

Most people are more familiar with cantharidin by its common name, Spanish fly. The substance is sold commercially as a powder with aphrodisiac properties, although its only known effect on humans is skin blistering. Spanish fly is produced by crushing blister beetles (in the family Meloidae), which make and secrete the substance. Fire-colored beetles do not make cantharidin as the blister beetles do, and scientists are still unsure whether they get the chemical from blister beetles or from some other source.

surface area for picking up odors, and are especially partial to foods that contain a chemical known as cantharidin. To tempt a female, the male lets her know that his diet includes this chemical by secreting a cantharidin-laced glob from his head, which the female promptly eats, according to

Left: In the genus *Nemognatha*, this blister beetle advertises its toxicity with its bright orange body. This and other beetles in the family Meloidae make and secrete a chemical that can cause a human's skin to blister. Strangely, the same chemical is marketed as an aphrodisiac.

Below: This native North American deathwatch beetle (*Euvrilletta peltata*, formerly classified in the genus *Xyletinus*), is sometimes known as a Virginia creeper death-watch beetle. Like other members of its family, it makes eerie ticking sounds in old wood, including the walls of some houses.

DEATHWATCH BEETLES

In years past, people would stay home and sit up through the night with a sick or dying friend or relative. Often, they would hear a soft tapping coming from the walls—the noise of the dreaded deathwatch beetle (in the family Anobiidae), which was counting down the patient's last minutes of life. This depiction of the beetle is hardly a fair one, especially since the beetle's taps have nothing to do with a human's lifespan, but everything to do with finding a mate. The typically dark-colored, 0.04-to-0.3 inch-long (1–8 mm) beetles live in old, often rotting wood and produce the sound by striking their heads against the lumber in an aging building's structure.

Night Lights

Known as a firefly or a lightning bug, this insect is actually one of a number of beetles (in the family Lampyridae) that can make its abdomen flash with light. Although a child may think otherwise, the insects are not lighting up for our benefit, but instead to find mates.

Beetle Code

Like a ship at night that pulses a Morse code with a spotlight, fireflies communicate through their flashes. The insect's glow is a cold light, called bioluminescence, produced when an enzyme mixes with oxygen and another chemical within an organ in the beetle's abdomen—a process the firefly can control. Scientists are intrigued by the insect's light production, which is amazingly energy-efficient. A typical lightbulb releases the bulk of its energy as heat rather than light, but a firefly's illumination is nearly 100 percent efficient and releases almost no heat.

Among most fireflies, the male produces a certain pattern of flashes that the female of its species recognizes. The female flashes back with a similarly distinctive signal to let the male know where she is. This back-and-forth light show continues as the male draws closer and closer, finally pinpointing the female and mating with her. The males of some species, including the North American species *Photinus carolinus,* along with several Asian species, flash in synchrony as if someone was flipping on and off a string of Christmas lights. Scientists are still unsure of the significance of the coordinated flashing.

Glowworms tend to do things a little differently. In the European species (*Lampyris noctiluca*), the females are the only ones that light up. The 0.6- to

During the day, people often overlook fireflies such as this one clinging to the underside of a leaf. On a summer's night, however, fireflies make their presence known with their distinctive yet ephemeral flashes.

"Before, beside us, and above, the firefly lights his lamp of love."

—BISHOP REGINALD HEBER

0.7-inch (1.5–1.8 cm) males have a typical firefly appearance with a large semicircle of a pronotum that covers the head, and a pair of long forewings, or elytra, that conceal the abdomen. The female is a bit larger at 0.6 to 1 inch (1.5–2.5 cm) long. Although she has the same pronotum, she is wingless. Females are typically called glowworms. During mating season, the females flash as the males observe from vegetation to select their mates. After copulating, the female lays her eggs and then dies.

Nefarious Flashes

Not all fireflies flash to find a mate. They flash to eat. According to a study at the University of Florida, a male firefly of the species *Photinus macdermotti* produces a two-flash pattern, and a female waits one second before responding with her own twinkle of light. Hungry females of other species in the genus *Photuris* not only know the male's pattern, but can also perfectly mimic the female's response flash. The copycat females lie in wait, drawing in the male with their flashes. By the time he finally arrives closely enough to discover the deception, it is often too late. The copycat female snatches the male and makes a meal of him.

Although many people call all firefly larvae glowworms, scientists often reserve the name "common glowworm" for one species, *Lampyris noctiluca*, which is found in Europe. Only the females have a strong glow, which they use to attract males.

SHINE ON

A good pair of sunglasses usually has polarizing filters on its lenses to block glare. For some butterflies, however, the glare is not only a good thing, but also a necessary cue for finding mates. Scientists at Duke University and the Smithsonian Tropical Research Institute found that the glint from the highly reflective wings of butterflies in the genus *Heliconius* helped males locate them for mating. The researchers discovered the importance of the iridescence by showing a flapping female wing to a male and observing his eager response. If they added a polarizing filter that eliminated the polarized light, and therefore the wing's shimmer, however, the males were far more likely to ignore the wing.

Some butterflies attract mates with not only the color of their wings, but also their shine. An example is this beautifully patterned female *Heliconius numata*, which lives in South America and is shown feeding from a neotropical *Psiguria* flower.

Mating "Songs"

The sounds produced by insects go far beyond cricket chirps and cockroach hisses. During courtship, different species drum, click, and squeal in mating "songs" to draw the opposite sex.

This young stonefly is not yet an adult, but when it finally matures and develops its long wings, its courtship will involve sound rather than looks. An adult male will advertise for a female's attention by drumming out a beat with his abdomen.

A Musical Phallus?

The pygmy water boatmen (in the family Micronectidae) are 0.08 inches (2 mm) or less in body length, but otherwise look similar to the much, much larger giant water bugs (of the family Belostomatidae). When viewed from above, both types of aquatic insects have an overall oval shape, two enlarged forelegs that they use as oars to thrust them through the water, and a pair of big eyes. Unlike the giant water bugs, male pygmy water boatmen produce sound in an unusual way. They make a series of soft chirps, not with a ridged plate on the abdomen, as scientists had once thought, but with the male sex organ, the aedeagus. A male's aedeagus is straddled by two tiny genital structures called parameres, and the aedeagus and the parameres are contained in a capsule. To make the female-drawing chirp, the male scrapes the capsule over one of the parameres. The profile of the paramere, which may have a sickled, lobed, or other shape, is one of the features scientists now use to tell apart the otherwise nearly identical species in this family.

Stonefly Drummers

Male stoneflies (in the order Plecoptera) pound out a beat to pick up females. Each male will drum his abdomen on the ground, a twig, or some other surface. In some species, the female responds with thumps of her own. After they come together on land and mate, the female soon flies to a nearby stream where she dips her abdomen and releases her eggs. The females of some species may sit on overhanging branches and let their eggs drop into the water.

Turning It Up

Peculiar-looking insects with robust front legs perfect for digging tunnels in the ground, mole crickets (in the family Gryllotalpidae) "sing" for their mates. A male has the file-and-scraper structures common to other crickets, and likewise uses them to produce his chirps. Most crickets make their calls from above-ground, but the mole cricket does his chirping under-ground. To ensure his song is loud enough to tempt a female, he creates megaphones, two tunnels shaped like funnels, that amplify the sound, pro-jecting it hundreds of yards.

Moth Castanets

Some moths have small knobby structures, called castanets, on their forewings. At the height of the upstroke during flight, the tops of their wings touch and the castanets click together. For some of these moths, the clicking sound protects them from bats, which use their echolocation skills to swoop down and eat moths. The ultrasonic sound produced by the moth's cas-tanets adequately confuses the bats. Australian male whistling moths (in the family Agaristidae) use clicks of their castanets to announce their avail-ability to females, and at the same time to make their presence known to other male whistling moths in the area.

SILENT MAJORITY

The field crickets (*Teleogryllus oceanicus*) on the Hawaiian island of Kauai have become unusually quiet. According to 2005 research at the University of California, Riverside, more than 9 in 10 male crickets now have mutant wings that are unable to produce the species' typical chirp. The researchers believe the population shift toward mute males arose in response to the arrival of parasitic flies (*Ormia ochracea*) that invaded Hawaii from North America and became prevalent in the 1990s. The flies lay their eggs on crickets, and the eggs hatch into larvae that eat the cricket from the inside. Because the flies find meals for their young by tracking the male crickets' sounds, their chirping has switched from a desirable trait for mating into a deadly liability for the caller, and the mutated-wing crickets now make up the silent majority.

Mole crickets have the same type of chirp-producing file and scraper that other crickets have, but they amplify their chirps, which they make underground, in an unusual way. The southern mole cricket (*Scapteriscus borellii*) pictured here is common to the southern United States.

Water Ripples

Ripples in the water are the equivalent of mating songs for two common aquatic insects. Both the water striders that skate across the water and the giant water bugs, also known as toe-biters, produce small ripples to "talk" to the opposite sex.

Water Striders

Although humans and water striders have coexisted on Earth for millennia, it has only been since the early 1970s that the insects' odd form of communication has been known. To make the ripples, the water striders hold their cigar-shaped bodies above the water and do push-ups with their legs. The motion generates ripples that flow outward from the feet much as a falling raindrop can cause a series of small, expanding, circular waves on the surface of the water.

The ripples visible around some of these water striders may be carrying an invitation to the opposite sex for a sexual rendezvous or a warning to competitors to stay away.

Researchers at the University of Binghamton in New York tested the ripple communication with a magnet and electrical setup that caused a water strider's leg to move and produce specific ripples, including those mimicking the pattern a male uses to announce his presence. The signals from at least one species (*Rhagadotarsus anomalus*) could draw females from a distance of two feet (61 cm) or more. The research also showed that some male striders (including *Gerris remigis*) changed their ripple pattern to a different, courtship mode when females approached closely enough. In at least two species (*R. anomalus* and *Tenogogonus albovittatus*), the females made responding courtship ripples. Researchers now know that male striders of several species make additional ripples, including vibrations produced during sex and after sex in at least one species (*R. anomalus*). In addition, males of many strider species generate ripples when they feel announcement vibrations from other males. These ripples are aggressive in nature and warn other males to stay away.

Giant Water Bugs and Whirligigs

Like the water striders, male giant water bugs do push-ups near the water surface to make ripples and communicate their in the western half of North America from the southern United States well into Canada.

When a male Mormon cricket is ready to mate, he begins chirping with the file and scraper on his diminutive wings and waits for a female to arrive. As she does, she climbs onto his back. The male then curls his abdomen upward, extends his aedeagus from the rear of his abdomen, and inserts it into the female's reproductive opening. Rather than conveying the sperm in loose form, the male Mormon cricket makes a spermatophore to contain the sperm and a little liquid, or seminal fluid. Glands in his body produce both the surrounding envelope of the spermatophore and proteins that go inside with the sperm and seminal fluid. Once the packet is prepared, the male conveys the entire thing to the female.

In the Mormon cricket, the male spermatophore can be huge, often 25 percent or more of his body weight. Despite the packet's size, it moves from the male's body to the female's in just a few minutes. Once he has made his delivery, the male's job is done. The sperm in the packet seeps into the female's reproductive tract, but the envelope and the rest of the spermatophore's contents do not go to waste. The female reaches down to the still partially protruding spermatophore and eats it, gaining some nourishment from it. The female could no doubt use the extra nutrition. A typical Mormon cricket female lays from several dozen to more than a hundred eggs.

When this male Mormon cricket mates with a female, he will pass a huge sperm packet—sometimes weighing a quarter of his overall body mass—into the female's reproductive tract. Unlike the male, the female has a long, blade-like ovipositor extending from the rear of her body.

DYING TO REPRODUCE

Tiny flies with a mosquitolike appearance, gall midges in the genus *Miastor*, are some of the few insects that can reproduce while they are still larvae. Instead of laying eggs, the mother larva retains them in her body. The eggs hatch there into new larvae, which survive by feasting on their mother's internal tissues, eventually killing her. The young finally emerge from their mother's hollow carcass and may either reproduce in the same manner or go on to pupate into an adult midge.

This scanning electron micrograph reveals the genitalia, or aedeagus, of a male blue-tailed damselfly (*Ischnura elegans*). The two hooklike extensions at the tip are sperm scoops that the male uses to enter the female and remove sperm that she may have obtained from a previous mating.

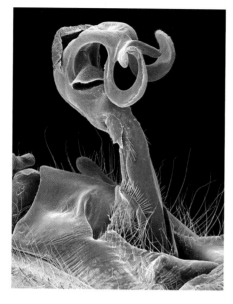

Unusual Reproductive Organs

Size matters . . . especially for the male rove beetle (*Aleochara tristis*). Adults are oblong with short elytra that resemble a shoulder jacket and leave the abdomen exposed. As occurs with most other insect species, the male copulates by everting his aedeagus, which is otherwise tucked away inside his body. What is different about the rove beetle's reproductive organ is its length—more than twice as long as his body. According to researchers at the University of Freiburg in Germany, the male has no problem inserting the ungainly organ into the female's reproductive tract, but has to take unusual means in order to put it away when he is finished mating. The researchers report that the beetle "shoulders" the organ by placing its midway point between the top of a wing and his pronotum, so he can retract it one half at a time and avoid tangling it.

Another insect with an unusually long phallus is the male earwig in the species *Euborellia plebeja*. Like the rove beetles, the earwigs have short elytra and exposed abdomens. A male of this earwig species has an aedeagus about the length of his 0.4-inch-long (1 cm) body, but it is very delicate and sometimes breaks off during mating. In this species, however, that does not mean the end of the individual's reproductive days. The male simply falls back on his spare, according to researchers at Tokyo Metropolitan University. Scientists had known for some time that these male earwigs had two sex organs, but they thought that the extra one was nonfunctional. The 2001 research, however, showed that the males could use the second organ to mate with females and fertilize their eggs.

Playing Pickup

Some male insects do not have to concern themselves with withdrawing an extremely long reproductive organ from a female's body because their organs do not have to go near her. Instead, these males leave their spermatophores lying about for the female to pick up herself. An example is the silverfish (order Thysanura). Silverfish are the typically small, flat, teardrop-shaped insects often seen speeding across a bathroom or basement floor. To mate, the male runs a length of silk, like a low clothesline, and places one of his spermatophores under it. He then guides the female to the silk thread, which she follows until she finds and retrieves his sperm packet.

Save It for a Rainy Day

In many insects, females do not necessarily have to fertilize their eggs immediately. They instead sock away the sperm in a storage organ, called the spermatheca, which is located deep within her reproductive tract. The females then release a little of the sperm at a time, so they can fertilize eggs over an extended period of time. Depending on the species, some females can continue fertilizing eggs from a single mating for several days, weeks, or even years.

As its name suggests, this male stalk-eyed fly (*Teleopsis dalmanni*) sees the world from protruding, sticklike appendages on its head. Females find large-stalked males to be especially alluring.

WIDE-EYED WONDERS

One of the strangest male enhancements occurs in the stalk-eyed flies. In this family (the Diopsidae), the male's two eyes are set on two long stalks, which separate them by a distance equal to or longer than its body length. A male displays his stalked eyes to face off for a food source. Usually just the sight of a longer-stalked fly is enough to send away a challenger, but if not, the two flies may wrestle. Stalk length also makes a difference to females; they prefer to mate with the widest-eyed males.

Assuring Paternity

In the insect world, a typical female mates several times with different males, often during a single breeding season. In such consecutive matings, new sperm cells enter her reproductive tract, commonly driving aside previous contributions from other males and taking over the prime position for fertilizing her eggs. The result is rather like a game of "king of the hill," with the males competing for the best shot at fathering young. In some cases, a female is able to pick and choose between sperm batches from different males, but often the onus falls on the male to improve his chances of passing on his genes.

Frequent Mating

For males of many species, the best way to hedge their bets in the sperm lottery is to play over and over again. With every mating, new sperm cells and other fluids from the male usually flush out at least some of the other sperm or remove it from the preeminent fertilizing location. If a male happens to be the last contributor before a female begins laying her eggs, his sperm are in good position to fertilize her eggs. This tactic also works well for those females that store the sperm in the spermatheca and mete it out to their eggs over a long period, sometimes their entire lifespans. In this case, sperm from a lucky male may fertilize eggs long after the mating act and sometimes long after he has perished.

Prolonged Coupling

Some males help assure the paternity of offspring by using their own bodies to block another male's access to a female. In other words, the male remains coupled with a female long after he has transferred his sperm, and therefore makes it difficult, if not impossible, for another male to mate with her. A pair of lovebugs, for instance, may be linked together for more than two days. Sightings of mating lovebugs, which couple at the abdomen with their bodies pointing in opposite directions, are so common in the southern United States that the insects are sometimes called two-headed bugs.

Once the mating process begins, a pair of love-bugs may remain linked together—abdomen to abdomen—for hours, even days. This prolonged joining, as seen in the pair at the center of the flower at right, has led to another nickname for the insects: two-headed bugs.

presence to the opposite sex. When a female responds and approaches a male, the two mate, and she lays her eggs soon after. For many male insects, this would be the end of the male's contribution to his offspring. This is not true of the giant water bugs. The unusual after-sex, and indeed after-

birth, participation by the father is described elsewhere in this book (see chapter 15).

Scientists are less sure about ripple communication in whirligigs, the small beetles that spin in circles on the surface of still water. They do know that the beetles use their ripples much the same way that a bat uses echolocation. A bat sends out sound waves that bounce off objects and return to it. By sensing and interpreting the return signals, the bat can locate prey very precisely. Whirligig beetles also sense prey, but with ripple vibrations instead of sound waves. Since the whirligigs have this communication system available to them, many scientists suspect that they also use their ripples for mating purposes.

Giant water bugs, also known as toe-biters, communicate via ripples in much the same way as water striders. The water vibrations are helpful for these insects, which often remain concealed in underwater vegetation. These hiding places provide an ideal location for ambushing prey.

LISTENING FOR BATS

Moths in the families Noctuidae and Arctiidae make no sounds, but they each have a pair of good-sized tympana on the thorax. Why? The moths are able to pick up the extremely high-pitched, echolocating squeals of bats, which are predators of moths. When the moths hear the squeals, they begin flying in erratic patterns that make them a more elusive target for the bats' sonar.

It may seem as if this grey dagger moth (*Acronicta psi*) would be an easy prey for a much swifter-flying bat, but the insect and other moths in the families Arctiidae and Noctuidae have found a way to confound the voracious mammals.

CHAPTER 14

INSECT MATING

A DESCRIPTION OF COPULATION among the insects would be much simpler if all insects mated the same way, but they do not. In many species, the male clambers onto the back of a female, bends his abdomen around so that the end of his and the end of hers meet, and they mate in this position. Other species mate with the female on top, or with the male and female pointing away from each other and only the tips of their abdomens touching. Males frequently have claspers to help them hang on to a female while they are copulating. These structures come in especially handy for insects that mate neither on the ground nor on plant stems and leaves, but in midair while flying. In some insects, mating is a private affair, with one male and one female coupling on their own. In others, however, mating swarms may be the norm, and dozens, even hundreds, of insects may mate at the same time.

The following pages explore just some of the tremendous diversity found among the insects, including the use of sperm packets, the diversity of tactics employed by males to ensure the paternity of a female's young, and the sometimes-dramatic differences between male and female insects.

Left: This pair of chalk-hill blue butterflies (*Lysandra coridon*) settles on a flower to mate. Inset: Dragonflies have an unusual mating style. The male (on top) stores his sperm forward on his body. To mate, this male blue dasher (*Pachydiplax longipennis*) grasps a female behind her head, and she curls her abdomen forward to retrieve the sperm.

Fertilization

In a common method of mating among insects, the male insect has genitalia, called an aedeagus, that he uses to deliver sperm directly into the reproductive tract of a female. Fertilization follows when an egg and sperm cell combine. Although this description could be lifted almost word for word and dropped into a primer on human reproduction, little else about insect mating transfers so easily—especially when the insects veer from this reproductive mode.

Sperm Packets in Crickets

One difference between two-legged and six-legged animals is the prevalence of sperm packets in the latter.

Sperm packets, known as spermatophores, occur in many insects. One is the Mormon cricket (*Anabrus simplex*), which also goes by the name western cricket.

Mormon crickets are actually katydids, although they look more like a cross between a grasshopper and a cricket. Adults come in several colors, including brown, black, and greenish tan, and usually grow to about an inch (2.5 cm) long. Unlike many other katydids, they have very short wings barely extending past the thorax, and they cannot fly at all. Females do, however, have the long swordlike ovipositor that is a typical feature of the katydid family (Tettigoniidae). Mormon crickets live

Like the Mormon crickets, these dead-leaf bush crickets (in the genus *Typophyllum*) are actually members of the katydid family. Photographed in the rain forest of Ecuador, the smaller male has just transferred a large white sperm packet to the female.

Another insect that regularly mates for prolonged periods is the eucalyptus snout beetle (*Gonipterus scutellatus*), a weevil originally from Australia but now living on many continents. Some matings in this species last for less than an hour, while others may extend for as long as two days. According to scientists from the University of Vigo in Spain, a long copulation does not always make fatherhood a certainty, because the female is able to select internally between the sperm from different males.

During the prolonged matings that occur in many species, the pair seldom remains stationary, and it is usually the female that drags the male around with her. Among the walking sticks, for example, the much-smaller male remains firmly attached to the female while she goes on with her daily routine.

Copulatory Plugs

The males of a number of species literally plug the opening to a female's reproductive tract after they have mated with her. The checkerspot butterfly (*Euphydryas chalcedona*) is an example. After mating, the male leaves behind extra mating fluids that harden into a plug, which is sometimes large enough to extend outside of her body. The plug, then, is a mechanical obstacle for subsequent males.

For honey bees (in the genus *Apis*), the male drones that mate with queens leave a copulatory plug made from more than secretions. During the mating process, his sex organs tear from his body and stay behind as the plug. Despite this extreme measure, a queen is often successful at removing the detached organ to make way for future matings.

Walkingsticks are another type of insect that may remain attached for long mating bouts. Photographed in the Amazon rain forest of Ecuador, a female carries on with her daily business while the much-smaller male clings to her back and continues mating.

A male checkerspot butterfly helps ensure that he will become a father by adding a hard plug to the female's reproductive opening after he has mated with her. This handsome butterfly is a member of the subspecies known as the Anicia checkerspot (*Euphydryas chalcedona anicia*).

Damselflies, such as this pair of banded demoiselles (*Calopteryx splendens*) mate in an unusual position. Male damselflies are also known for the efficient structures on their genitalia that can remove sperm from a female's previous matings before he copulates with her.

The male cowpea weevil (*Callosobruchus maculatus*), shown below in this scanning electron micrograph, has a spike-tipped aedeagus that not only delivers sperm, but also inflicts great damage to the female's reproductive tract. Female bean weevils typically mate just once in a lifetime.

Sperm Scoops

Among some insect species, the males endeavor not to keep other males away, but to eliminate the contribution from a previous male's sperm by removing it. One of the sperm-scooping species is the ebony jewelwing (*Calopteryx maculata*), a damselfly with smoky wings and a metallic-looking body. Part of the male's aedeagus is fashioned into a scraping device that clears previous sperm from a female's reproductive tract before he adds his own.

Sperm removal can be very effective. According to a study at the University of Sheffield in the United Kingdom, paternity was practically guaranteed for the last-copulating males in the damselfly species *Calopteryx splendens*. Although this male's sperm scoop is usually not able to remove every last bit of the previous sperm in a female's reproductive tract before he releases his own, the researchers found that 98 percent of a female's offspring are fathered by her last suitor.

Doing Damage

Some males use what may seem an even more underhanded method of ensuring that their sperm are the ones doing the fertilizing. Their reproductive organs have barbs, spines, and other destructive accoutrements that cause so much damage to the female's body that she either has difficulty mating again or cannot re-mate at all. One such male is the cowpea weevil (*Callosobruchus maculatus*). According to researchers also at the University of Sheffield, the male weevil's aedeagus is tipped with dozens of sharp spikes that tear at the female's reproductive tract. Although the female is usually able to shorten the encounter by kicking at the male, she still sustains significant injuries.

Sexual Stabbing

Mating in bedbugs (family Cimidae) can only be described as bizarre. The male delivers his sperm not through the female's normal reproductive opening, which she possesses and uses for laying her eggs, but through her abdominal wall. He accomplishes this feat by using his daggerlike aedeagus to stab into her body and release his sperm, a process that may result in both infections and significant physical damage to the female. To make matters worse for the female, she may have numerous mating partners during her lifetime.

Bedbugs are not the only insects that employ this method, which is appropriately called traumatic insemination. Other true bugs puncture the female's body during copulation, and the male of one species (*Xylocoris maculipennis*) may even grab, stab, and deliver his sperm into another male. The misplaced sperm may still make it to the correct target if the male "victim" goes on to mate with a female, because he may not only transfer his own sperm but also that of his "attacker."

OFF WITH HIS HEAD

Mating in praying mantids can be deadly. During copulation, a female mantid may chomp off the head of her male partner. Although this would bring the encounter to a premature end for most animals, among mantids it adds zest. With his head removed, the male mantid's body continues to gyrate, often more energetically, and, if appropriately inserted, releases his sperm. The female gains not only fertilization for her eggs, but also a full belly.

Reproduction can be hazardous for some males, too. A female praying mantid, the larger of the two in this mating pair, will sometimes eat the male's head during their sexual encounter.

Midair Mating

Most insect pairs mate while they are on the ground, on a branch, or attached to some other object. A number of insects, however, are able to copulate in midair. Most people are familiar with the periodic swarms of flying ants, which are actually the reproductive females and males engaging in a nuptial flight. Some additional insects that mate during flight include the caddisflies, dragonflies and damselflies, and certain wasps.

Caddisflies

Caddisflies are mothlike as adults, and swoop over ponds and lakes to mate and lay their eggs. The mating process begins when the female releases a pheromone and the male tracks its trail to the waiting female. Although they can mate while on the ground or on vegetation, pairs frequently mate during flight. Afterward, the female lays her eggs on, near, and sometimes in the water. The eggs hatch into aquatic larvae that often survive in silken cases. They transform into adults after going through a pupal stage. Adults live only a week or two, and they spend most of that time reproducing.

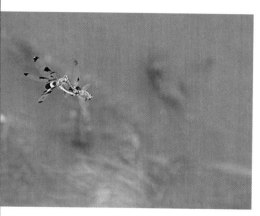

Above: This male dragonfly is using devices called claspers at the end of his abdomen to grab a female behind her head. Now that he has a hold, she will draw up the tip of her own abdomen to reach a sperm pouch on his abdomen just behind his thorax.

Tiphiid Wasps

The females of certain wasps in the family Tiphiidae are wingless, but this does not stop them from mating in midair. The male, which has wings and can fly, catches the scent of a pheromone the female releases, and *à la* Superman and Lois Lane, flies to her and whisks her off the ground. The pair mates in the air, and the male returns her to earth, where she selects a site to lay her eggs. She commonly opts for another insect, usually a beetle, as a birthing location. She stings the beetle, which paralyzes it, and lays her eggs on its body. When they hatch, her larvae find plenty of food in the body of their indisposed host.

Dragonflies and Damselflies

Other unusual midair maters are the dragonflies and damselflies, the two groups in the order Odonata. Males have copulatory structures that make possible a unique mating procedure. A male dragonfly or damselfly produces sperm at the rear of his abdomen, but instead of delivering it straightaway to the female as is common in many insects, he first transfers it to a sperm pouch on the underside of his abdomen near his thorax. Once he has the sperm in storage, he approaches a female and grabs her from above and just behind her head with pincerlike

Male hover flies (in the family Syrphidae) use their ability to hover in flight to court females. In fact, several males may competitively hover over a female. Here, a male (top) has won the attention of a female and the two are mating in midair.

claspers at the end of his abdomen. Copulation proceeds when she bends her abdomen forward to align her reproductive opening with his sperm pouch, and he begins delivering his sperm. Often, the attachment of the female's reproductive organ to the male's pouch can be quite a challenge for her, and she may need to make numerous attempts before securing a good connection. The strange mating position does not prohibit the insects from taking to the air, and the pair may fly while continuing to copulate.

MAN-MADE FLIES

In fly-fishing, an angler uses a long, flexible rod to cast a line and an artificial lure, called a fly. Success requires both skill and the right sort of lure. Often, lures resemble the type of aquatic insect that is hatching at the time of the fishing expedition. Some anglers tie their own flies, blending a combination of such materials as feathers, tufts of fur, and pieces of tinsel to mimic the wings and other body parts of an insect.

Anglers sometimes craft their own lures, such as these, called "flies," to attract a bite from a trout or other game fish. When these lures are expertly dangled from the end of a fishing rod, they look enough like a prey item to fool a passing fish.

Mating Swarms

In the spring of each year, residents along the shores of Lake St. Clair in Michigan are inundated with mayflies, all of which are looking for mates. The soft-bodied flying insects cover the ground, windowpanes, the sides

Europe's burrowing mayfly (*Ephemera danica*) has the typical mayfly features: a pair of large forewings, a pair of much smaller, triangular-shaped hind wings and long filamentous cerci extending from the rear of the abdomen.

of buildings, and anywhere else they can find to land. During these periods, it is common to see a person walking down the street with several mayflies clinging to his or her clothing and hair. The insects, which are sometimes called fishflys, also gather in the evening around streetlights, and can so thickly cover the street at intersections that their car-crushed bodies slicken the road and cause accidents. This same scene is repeated in areas around freshwater nearly the world over.

This yellow mayfly (*Heptagenia sulphurea*) sits on a riverside stone. After mating, the females of the species will fly back to the water, where they will lay their eggs before dying.

Life Cycle

Mayflies live up to three years as naiads, aquatic nymphs that survive underwater. The nymphs have little resemblance to the adults. An adult mayfly has a stick-thin body, large forewings, and short hind wings; a naiad has no wings and a series of flaplike gills that extend from the sides of its abdomen. The mayfly is the only insect that develops functioning wings before it becomes an adult. The naiad has one final stage, called the subimago, immediately preceding its adult, or imago, phase. The subimago mayfly closely resembles an adult, but it has smaller legs and wings, the filaments extending from its abdomen are shorter, and its reproductive structures are not fully developed. The wings of the subimago usually have a darker color than those of the adults, and the hue and pattern of the body is typically less pronounced.

At the adult stage, most mayflies have nonfunctional mouthparts, so they cannot eat. This does not present a problem, however, because their time on Earth is fleeting. As their scientific name reflects (the order is called Ephemeroptera), they consequently have only one thing on their minds: reproducing.

Copulation Congregation

A few mayfly species have adults that live to the ripe old age of three days, but most perish within 24 hours. During their very short adulthood,

The transformation from subimago to a sexually mature adult, called an imago or spinner, is a vulnerable time for a mayfly. Here, a newly transformed imago rests next to the discarded shell of its subimago phase.

SPECIFICATIONS

Insects: Mayflies
Order: Ephemeroptera
Meaning of Ephemeroptera: refers to their ephemeral, or short-lived, winged, adult phase, which typically lasts only a day or two
Typical characteristics of adults in this order:
- large, triangular-shaped forewings with much smaller hind wings (if present)
- net-veined, transparent wings that are held together and above the body when at rest
- long, soft body
- front legs that are typically held forward and are sometimes mistaken for antennae by humans
- two tiny antennae and two large eyes on the head
- two long, threadlike cerci and often a third tail filament between them
- the larvae are called naiads and are aquatic; the adults are terrestrial

DIVERSITY
Number of known species: about 2,000
Size: The smallest mayfly species are about 0.04 inches (1 mm) in body length. The largest mayflies are species from Madagascar in the genus *Proboscidoplocia*. Some have body lengths of 2 to 3 inches (5.1–7.6 cm).
Sampling of benefits to humans: Mayfly naiads serve as bioindicators of the health of a pond, lake, or stream. Adults and naiads are also an important food source for many other animals.

they must mate and lay their eggs. By emerging from the water together and forming massive swarms, they greatly improve the chances that they will find mates before their life clocks run out. The swarms themselves consist mainly of males. When a female sees the swarm, which is usually dark with thousands of flying males, she flies toward it. The first male to reach her will grasp her, usually from below, by clamping his especially long front legs up and around her thorax. He then bends up his abdomen to align his reproductive parts with hers for midair mating. This is the grand finale for the male, and he dies shortly thereafter, his soft body quickly drying out and shriveling into a shadow of his former self. The female has one more task. She holds death at bay until she can return to the water to lay her eggs. Often, the female dies within moments of the last eggs emerging from her body.

Male versus Female

Right: Among some dragonflies, one sex in the species may have additional markings. *Libellula pulchella,* or twelve-spotted skimmer, is an example. Both sexes sport 12 dark spots: 3 on each wing. Males, however, also have 2 extra white spots on each wing.

Below: This mating pair of green darner dragonflies (*Anax junius*) illustrates the difference between the sexes. The male (at right) has a sky-blue abdomen. The female's abdomen, which is below the water's surface, is purplish gray.

Male and female insects often look so much alike that they are difficult if not impossible to tell apart. In some species, however, even a novice can readily recognize an insect's sex. The moths and the earwigs, as described earlier, are two groups of insects that usually have readily identifiable genders. Male moths typically have much larger and more elaborate antennae, which are well suited to perceive pheromones produced by the females, and male earwigs commonly have bigger and more curved cerci than the opposite sex.

Dragonflies

Both the sperm-storage organ behind the thorax and end-of-the-abdomen claspers are indicative of male dragonflies, but the gender differences do not end there. Often, male and female dragonflies have color variations that are apparent even from a distance. Two common North American dragonfly species that display this disparity between genders, called sexual dimorphism, are the twelve-spotted skimmer (*Libellula pulchella*) and the green darner (*Anax junius*). Adult twelve-spotted skimmers are large dragonflies, typically 2 to 2.25 inches (5–5.7 cm) in body length. Both sexes have three dark spots on each wing, but the males typically have an additional pair of white spots on each wing. Green darners are even larger dragonflies with bodies that grow to about 3 inches (7.6 cm) long.

Both males and females have clear wings, except for a small box of color near the tips, and a grass green thorax. The two sexes are easily distinguishable, however, by the color of the abdomen. A female's abdomen is purplish gray, and a male's is deep sky blue.

Stag beetles (in the family Lucanidae) have pronounced differences between males and females. The male, such as the one above, typically has far more massive jaws than the female.

Velvet Ants

Although they are wasps, the common name of velvet ants is not completely off base. The males do indeed look like wasps, but the females are wingless and fuzzy insects that give the impression of velvet-covered ants. Like many, although not all other bees and wasps, the females have another feature the males do not: an ovipositor that is modified into a stinger.

Leaf-footed Bugs

Many male leaf-footed bugs have enlarged and either ornamented or armed hind legs that set them apart from their female counterparts. One such species is *Nematopus indus*, which has a green thorax, long black-and-white antennae, and black-and-green patterned front wings. The male also possesses beefed-up hind legs armed with hefty, curved spines. The males of this and other leaf-footed bugs show off their hind legs to other males, sometimes getting into wrestling matches, to gain or maintain access to females.

Insect "Antlers"

A few insects have head ornaments comparable to the antlers of a male deer or elk: the males with the largest ornaments usually can convince other males to back off. Some males have ornaments that look like bottle openers, and they use them to lever another male off of a female in the same way that a bottle opener pries the cap off of a cola bottle. Stag beetles (in the family Lucanidae) are examples of insects with large male ornaments, actually their jaws. In the larger species, the male has enormous jaws that he will use, if necessary, to discourage other males' advances on a female.

CHAPTER 15

EGG LAYING

THE JOB OF AN INSECT PARENT may carry great responsibility or it may hold very little. An example of the low-duty end of the spectrum is the male damselfly. He delivers his sperm to the female during mating and then makes no other contribution to the offspring. A female damselfly does only a bit more. She lays her eggs and then promptly leaves the scene. She is not unusual, however—a great many female insects abandon their eggs after laying them. This does not mean that the eggs are left out in the open for any passing predator to devour. Many mothers select locations that offer varying degrees of protection for the eggs or larvae, or perhaps a food source for the hatching larvae. A variety of species help to construct their own nurseries, some by making silk-and-plant bags and others by bubbling up excreted plant juices around themselves. Numerous insect larvae also produce chemicals that trigger plant cells to proliferate around them to not only provide shelter but also to give them something to eat as they grow. Nests, too, serve as havens for larvae, and although they are not foolproof, they do confer a measure of protection to otherwise vulnerable offspring.

Left: A male damselfly still clings to the female as she dips the end of her abdomen in the water to lay her eggs. Once the egg-laying is complete, the parents leave the scene, and the eggs are on their own. Inset: Located under a flowerpot, this ant nest contains hundreds of whitish to translucent eggs. Ants rush among the eggs, and if the nest is left exposed, they carry the eggs to a safer location.

Nurseries

Background: A typical cattail in the genus *Typha* has an oblong brown seed head that will disperse its seeds in the fall. Because of the work of certain moth caterpillars, however, some retain their fluffy seeds and serve as a warm nursery for growing insects.

Not quite living in the full-scale nests of the highly social bees and wasps, but not completely homeless either, many insect eggs and larvae have at least some protection from predators and the elements during their development. Cattail moths, bagworm moths, and spittlebugs are but a few examples.

Cattail Moths

Cattails, commonly seen in North American marshes and along pond edges, sometimes look as if they have partially exploded from their normal firm, brown, cigar-shaped seed heads into whitish wads of fluff. The culprit behind the plump bundles is often the larvae of the cattail moth, *Limnaecia phragmitella*. The adult moths are small, beige insects with narrow antennae and wingspans of just 0.4 to 0.8 inches (1–2 cm). Adult females lay their eggs on tall plants, including brush-topped reeds called *Phragmites*, and cattails (*Typha* species). Before settling inside the cattail head, the hatching caterpillars spin silk around it. Normally, the cattail head sheds its seeds at the end of the season, but the silk-wrapped heads cannot. Instead, the seeds and the fine threads attached to them remain on the stalks to provide fluffy insulation to the cattail moth larvae living inside.

MILLIONS AND MILLIONS OF EGGS

An ant from Africa may well hold the record for producer of the most eggs by an individual. The queen ant of the African driver ant (*Dorylus wilverthi*) reportedly lays eggs at the astonishing rate of three or four million eggs every 25 days. The worker ants in the colony usually range from 0.1 to 0.4 inches (0.3–1 cm) long, but the queen may be 2 inches (5.1 cm) long or more.

Bagworm Moths

The caterpillar of a bagworm moth (*Thyridopteryx ephemeraeformis*) gathers pine needles, pieces of twigs and bark, and other debris, and spins its collection with silk to fashion it into a long, thin bag. It then lives inside, poking its head and front legs out of one end to nibble at leaves. The other end of the bag, which is also open, allows its feces to drop clear. When the time comes, the caterpillar seals shut its bag and pupates there, soon metamorphosing into an adult. The adult male is a dark-bodied moth with long, clear forewings and smaller hind wings. An adult female, on the other hand, retains her caterpillar features, never gaining legs, wings, or antennae. She stays inside the bag throughout her lifetime, releasing pheromones, which draw males for breeding. After mating, she lays her eggs inside the bags and dies shortly thereafter. The eggs spend the winter in the protective bag, hatch out the following spring, and the young caterpillars leave to begin making their own bags.

Spittlebugs

A spittlebug, the common name for the larva of many froghoppers (true bugs in the family Cercopidae), is responsible for much of the moist froth that people see dangling from grass blades and plant and tree stems in warm months. After hatching, the typical froghopper larva produces a secretion from its anus and blows air into it to turn it into a white foam. The secretion is mainly excess liquid left over from its diet of plant sap. Inside this frothy nursery, the larva

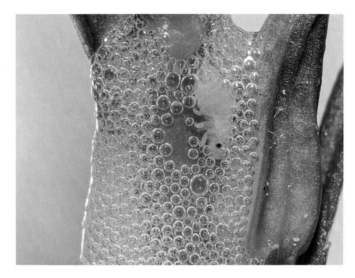

remains unseen by predators while continuing to feed on the plant's juices.

Although most people call all froth-producing froghopper larvae "spittlebugs," entomologists usually save the name for one species, the froghopper *Cephisus siccifolius* that occurs from Mexico to South America. Their larvae, too, make their own bubbly nurseries.

Above: Young froghoppers make their own nurseries by blowing bubbles into a liquid that they secrete from the anus. This froghopper nymph, known as a meadow spittlebug (*Philaenus spumarius*) is barely visible in its foamy home.

Above left: The caterpillar of the bagworm moth combines its silk with a collection of pine needles, twigs, and other items to shape a bag, where it then lives. The adult female looks much like the caterpillar and also remains inside her bag.

A MOTHER'S "MILK"

Human and other mammal mothers produce milk to sustain their infants. Certain insect mothers, too, produce food for their growing larvae. These include the tsetse flies (in the family Glossinidae, genus *Glossina*), which are found in Africa. Eggs hatch inside the mother, and the larvae survive and grow there on nutritional meals produced by the mother's internal glands. Once born, the larvae pupate and finally become adults. Unlike many other insect females that have scores—and sometimes hundreds of thousands—of offspring during their lives, a female tsetse fly typically has only a handful. Tsetse flies are most known, however, for spreading trypanosomiasis, or sleeping sickness, in humans. According to the World Health Organization, at least 60,000 people die from the disease each year.

Egg Dumping

Female water bugs put their eggs in an unusual spot: on the body of their mates. This male water bug is carrying a back full of them. A close look reveals that some of the eggs have already hatched.

Like many other bugs, eggplant lace bugs (*Gargaphia solani*) guard eggs and nymphs, but not always their own. This is because some lace bugs engage in "egg dumping," the practice of laying eggs on an existing egg pile from another female, who then guards the whole mass. This frees up the first female to lay additional eggs elsewhere. Sometimes, however, the egg-dumping female will take over the egg pile from its initial owner, who then starts a fresh egg mass elsewhere.

In some insects, including certain species of assassin bugs, the females rely not on other females to raise their young, but on their mates as well as other passing males. The males take over egg-rearing duties and will roost over the brood to protect them from potential predators. The male typically stays with the eggs until they hatch and, depending on the species, may also remain for a while with the larvae.

Mr. Mom

Female water bugs (species in the genus *Belostoma*) expect more than egg-sitting duties from their mates. The females glue their eggs onto the male's back, or more accurately onto his forewings, which he then keeps folded down on his back. Despite the weight and cumbersomeness of the eggs, he carries them with him until they hatch. He is not as agile when he is laden with eggs and is therefore not as efficient a predator, but the effort pays off when he is able to pass on his genes to the next generation.

The female golden egg bug (*Phyllomorpha laciniata*) is less discriminating. This small, spiny-edged, white and dark brown bug will lay her eggs on plants, where they remain unguarded, or on the back of either a male or a female of her species. The carriers do not seem to mind if the eggs are not theirs and will carry them until they hatch. According to research at the Museo Nacional de Ciencias Naturales in Madrid, carried eggs are better protected from predators, and when given the choice, females opt to lay their eggs on the backs of other golden egg bugs.

Above: Hardly parent-of-the-year material, some female eggplant lace bugs are perfectly willing to add their eggs to another female's batch and quietly slip away. The intricate, lacelike wings visible in this adult are characteristic of other species in the lace bug family (Tingidae).

Left: Scientists believe that dragonflies, such as this one photographed in a Rio de Janeiro botanical garden, may lay their eggs on the hood or roof of a shiny car, mistaking it for the surface of a lake or pond.

PAINT-DESTROYING INSECT EGGS

In 2001, researchers at the University of São Paulo in Brazil pinned the blame for poor car paint finishes on dragonfly eggs. According to their study, dragonflies confuse the shiny finish on new, dark-colored cars with the water where they normally lay their eggs. When a dragonfly lays its eggs on a dark car that has been warmed to a high temperature by the sun, acid in the eggs can begin to eat away at the paint job in as little as three hours' time.

Nests

N ests are not especially common among the insects, but they are nonetheless familiar sights, especially among the ants, bees, and wasps of the order Hymenoptera. Although some members of this order do not build nests, many of them do, and some of these are elaborate structures.

Ant Colonies

As social insects, ants live in colonies and divide the work among the members, a select few of which handle reproduction. The remaining inhabitants take care of all other duties, including food gathering, defense, care of the reproductive caste and their offspring, and nest building. Depending on the species, ant nests may be a series of interconnecting tunnels and chambers underground or within wood.

Nests of the Florida harvester ant (*Pogonomyrmex badius*), for example, are subterranean and consist of horizontal chambers that veer off downward-sloped shafts. According to 2004 research at Florida State University, the brick-red ants make room for a growing population by increasing the size of existing chambers while adding new chambers deeper underground. A typical established colony has a nest ranging from 6.6 to 9.8 feet (2–3 m) deep.

Paper Wasps

Several species in the genus *Polistes* are commonly called paper wasps. Most adults are an inch (2.5 cm) long or less, and may be brown or reddish with yellow markings. Paper wasps build their nests with a building material they prepare themselves by chewing on wood fragments. The wood combines with their saliva to create a pastelike substance that eventually hardens into a papery product. Once the wasps find a suitable spot, often under a roof eave or in some other place that is protected from the weather, they begin by constructing a thin hanger, called a pedicel, to support the nest that will

Right: This European paper wasp (*Polistes gallicus*) builds its wood-and-saliva nest "upside down," with the cells visible from below.

Below: In 2003, the ill-fated space shuttle *Columbia* carried 15 harvester ants as part of an experiment developed by high school students and scientists to learn about ant-tunnel formation in low-gravity conditions. Here, the ants tunnel not in sand but through gel suitable to the rigors of space travel.

hang below it. The nest is a collection of vertical cells made with the same wood-saliva mix. Some species leave the cells exposed, but others lay a final sheet of "paper" over the bottom of the nest and provide only one hole for entry and exit.

Mud Daubers

Another nest that sometimes appears around homes is that of the mud dauber wasp, the name given to one of several species that build their nests of mud. Two of them, *Trypoxylon politum* and *Trypoxylon clavatum* are solitary wasps that share the common name organpipe mud dauber. The name

describes their mud nest, which is a number of long, abutting tubes that resemble miniature organ pipes. The adult mud daubers, black insects about 0.5 to 0.75 inches (1.3–1.9 cm) long, build their nests from mud that they collect and carry to the nest site, often under a porch overhang or a roof eave. Each "pipe" is separated into individual cells, and each cell contains one egg and one or more paralyzed spiders that the female collects for her soon-to-hatch larva to consume. While she is away, the male guards the nest. This is unusual among the wasps; nests are usually female-only projects.

The several species of wasps that build their nests of mud are called mud daubers. The building materials are clumps of mud that the wasps find and carry to the construction site.

CARPENTER BEES

Dark, shiny, and up to an inch (2.5 cm) long, eastern carpenter bees (*Xylocopa virginica*) provide parental care for their young. The female chews away half-inch-wide (1.3 cm), round tunnels into the timber of a house or other wood, although she does not eat the wood. She then adds an egg and a supply of bee bread to the farthest recesses of the tunnel, seals them into a chamber, and starts work on the adjacent chamber. The result is a succession of chambers, called brood cells, with each containing an egg and bee bread. As the eggs hatch, the larvae feed on the bee bread until they are ready to pupate, and then gnaw out of their cells. The oldest larvae, which were laid the farthest from the nest exit, end up emerging from the nest later than the youngest.

Carpenter bees chew into wood to make tunnels for their eggs. Damage from the tunneling is usually minimal, but over many years it can become extreme. This hole-riddled wood is the work of the carpenter bee species *Xylocopa caffra*.

Galls

The lumps, bumps, fingerlike projections, balls, and other abnormal outgrowths found on the leaves and stems of wildflowers, trees, shrubs, and other plants are often the result of insects. On almost any walk through a meadow, in a forest, or along a shoreline, a person can find a great number and variety of these outgrowths, called galls, and if the timing is right, can split one open to find an insect larva still living inside. Many insect orders contain gall-making species. These include Coleoptera (the beetles), Diptera (the flies), Hemiptera (including the aphids), Hymenoptera (including the sawflies and wasps), Lepidoptera (moths and butterflies), and Thysanoptera (the thrips).

In many cases, the galls begin to form as the result of chemicals imparted to the plant by an insect, which may be the mother as she is laying her eggs, or the offspring themselves. The chemicals trigger the plant tissue in the surrounding area to proliferate and form a tumorlike enlargement. The galls provide shelter as well as a ready food source for the growing larvae. The offspring eventually emerge from the gall, usually through a small exit hole, when they reach adulthood.

Goldenrod Galls

Goldenrod (*Solidago canadensis*) is the yellow-topped wildflower that many people blame for their late-summer hay fever. Goldenrod does not deserve the blame, however, because it is the simultaneously, but far less conspicuously flowering ragweed (*Ambrosia* species) that is usually responsible for the allergic reaction. Goldenrod is, nonetheless, interesting for its galls. Frequently, almost every plant has at least one large, firm gall on its stem. These galls may be round or elliptical, and typically about an inch (2.5 cm) in diameter. Sometimes, a single plant

These pink puffballs on a dog rose (*Rosa canina*) are galls caused by a rose gall wasp (*Diplolepsis rosae*). Female wasps lay their eggs in the rosebuds, which develop into the galls as the hatching wasp larvae develop inside.

stem will have one of each: a round gall and an elliptical gall separated by a couple of inches. A different insect is responsible for each of the two galls. A fly is associated with the spherical gall, and a moth with the elliptical version.

The goldenrod gall fly (*Eurosta solidaginis*) is a tiny, brown fly that reaches less than 0.2 inches (about 4–5 mm) in body length as an adult. The male sits in a prominent spot on the plant in the spring and performs a ritual dance of sorts to attract a female. After they mate, the female moves onto the stem, slices into it with her ovipositor, and lays her eggs. The eggs hatch about a week and a half later, and the larvae nibble away at the stem's interior, leaving behind a bit of their saliva. The saliva contains the chemicals that stimulate the plant cells to multiply, and a gall soon begins to

enlarge around one of the larvae. The larva remains inside the gall through the fall and winter, pupates the following spring, and finally emerges.

The goldenrod elliptical-gall moth (*Gnorimoschema gallaesolidaginis*) has a slightly different life cycle. A female lays her eggs in the fall rather than the spring and places each egg on a leaf instead of inside the stem. The egg remains on the leaf until it hatches the next spring. The larva creeps to a flower bud on the plant and munches its way through the bud and into the stem, where a gall forms. The larva pupates inside the gall and finally emerges in late summer to autumn as an adult moth.

This mango leaf is marked by a number of small bumps called galls. Various pests can cause galls on different types of plants, and some of the pests are insects.

Galls can take many shapes. They may be round, pointed on one end, oval, flattened, spine-covered, or any number of other shapes.

PUTTING GALLS TO USE

For centuries, humans have been extracting tannic acid from oak apple galls. Early on, Greeks used the tannic acid from certain galls, called Aleppo galls (from the oak tree *Quercus infectoria*) to dye wool and hair, and in various mixtures as first aid for burns and as a treatment for fevers. For hundreds of years, people used a permanent and water-resistant writing ink, called iron gall-nut ink, which was made in part from the galls' tannic acid. The treasuries of many countries, including the United States, England, and Germany, once printed their paper money with this ink. Since the middle of the twentieth century, however, other inks have taken its place as writing and printing media.

Although it is less commonly seen than the round and elliptical galls, a third gall often strikes goldenrod, but it has a completely different appearance. This gall is a clump of closely growing leaves taking over a spot where a bud would otherwise be. Called a goldenrod bunch gall, it is the result of another species of insect, a midge known as *Rhopalomyia solidaginis* (in the family Cecidomyiidae).

Oak Apple Gall

People frequently find oak apple galls—lightweight, tan or brown spheres—lying on woodland trails. When they break open the galls, they find a lattice of stiff threads inside. The galls, which occur on oak trees and may be nearly the size of golf balls, are the larval homes for several different gall wasp species. In Europe, the common oak apple gall wasp is the species *Biorhiza pallida*, which has a two-part life history. In part one, the female lays her eggs in the spring, inserting them into a bud on the oak tree. The larvae spur the development of the oak apple gall, which forms on the tree's young leaves by midsummer. Shortly thereafter, mature and winged male and female wasps emerge and mate. Although scientists are unsure why, most galls produce only one sex:

Many of the tiny wasps in the family Cynipidae can produce galls on oak trees. These apple-colored galls, called oak apple galls, are the result of a gall-wasp infestation. Soon, the galls will turn tan or brown and drop to the ground. The wasp larva inside will soon metamorphose and emerge.

If willows are broad-leaved trees that lack the needles and cones of pine trees, why does this willow tree have a cone? It is a gall caused by a midge (a type of tiny fly). The female lays an egg on the tree's developing leaf bud. The emerging larva releases a chemical that stimulates the tree to develop the cone-shaped structure, called a willow pinecone gall.

all males or all females. In the second part of their life history, the newly mated females burrow down into the ground and lay their eggs in the roots of the tree. All of these eggs will become females. The roots form galls, too, although people rarely see them unless they are digging into the soil. The hatched larvae survive in the root gall for more than a year, and exit in late winter as wingless female wasps that begin climbing up the tree's trunk. These females reproduce parthenogenetically (without a male's input) and lay their eggs in the leaf bud of an oak tree, setting the stage for a new round of male-female mating. This switch

from one form of reproduction in one generation to another in the next— sexual to asexual—is appropriately called alternation of generations.

Willow Pinecone Gall

Shrubby willows (in the genus *Salix*) frequently spring up around shore-lines, and often bear what appear to be small pinecones. These cone-shaped structures are also galls, and the responsible insect is a midge, *Rabdophaga strobiloides*, the larva of which stimulates the plant to develop the gray gall. The larva remains inside over the winter, and then pupates and emerges in the spring.

CHAPTER 16

INSECT DEVELOPMENT

SCHOOLCHILDREN IN CLASSROOMS the world over have watched mesmerized as a fuzzy caterpillar placed in a jar goes through its changes to ultimately become a stunning butterfly. Even for jaded scientists, the transformation is indeed astonishing.

Not all insects have such an awe-provoking path to adulthood, but they are no less interesting. Some of the seemingly primitive insects, those that still have many of the characteristics of their ancestors, hatch from eggs into larvae that change very little as they grow into adults. These primitive species are all wingless, and include the bristletails, silverfish, and firebrats. All other insects either have wings or have lost their wings secondarily, which means that their ancestors had wings but they no longer do. Among this large group are insects with one of two major types of development. Many species, including dragonflies, grasshoppers, cockroaches, and earwigs, share a three-stage development that proceeds from egg to larva to adult. Butterflies and moths have one more stage in their development: the pupa that falls between larva and adult. Other insects—such as beetles, flies, ants, and bees— also grow through a four-stage developmental process.

Left: This composite photograph shows a monarch butterfly (*Danaus plexippus*) leaving the case of its pupal stage, or chrysalis. As it emerges, the wings are soft and wrinkled, but abdominal fluids begin pumping into the wing veins, expanding them to full size. When the wings dry and harden, the butterfly can flutter away. Inset: The monarch caterpillar goes through several molts as it grows. Eventually, it will look for a place to pupate, the last stage before it transforms into a winged adult.

Gradual Development

Primitive insects, such as this firebrat, develop gradually, changing little even when they metamorphose into adults. They, along with the similarly wingless silverfish and bristletails, continue molting after they become adults. Winged insects, on the other hand, do not molt again once they have their wings.

Larval development occurs through a series of steps, called instars, that are separated by molts. During the molt, an insect sheds its old shell, or cuticle, and develops a new one.

Instars and Molting

To prepare for the molt, also known as ecdysis, an insect begins amplifying the volume of its hemolymph, or "blood," by retaining extra water from its food. It further expands its body at the time of molting by gulping air. In addition, it attaches its old cuticle to the ground, a stem, a leaf, or some other substrate to assist in its escape. Its expanding body helps to split the old cuticle, which separates along weak spots (often along the back of the thorax), and the insect contorts its body to rise up and out of the cuticle. People often find old, empty cuticles where the insects left them. Old cuticle can also be lost from insect gut or the inner walls of the tracheael (breathing) system during molts.

The insect's new cuticle needs a little time to spread out to its full size and to harden. This is a vulnerable stage for the insect, which is soft and usually white or light-colored until its cuticle hardens and takes on its normal color. Once the new cuticle

A cicada as it breaks free from the shell, or cuticle, of its last nymphal stage. Depending on the species, cicadas may spend up to 17 years as underground-living nymphs before becoming adults.

EVERY 17 YEARS . . .

Unlike many of the other true bugs, cicadas spend most of their lives underground. There, the nymphs feed on sap from tree roots and ever so slowly develop. In fact, nymphal development can take 4 to 17 years, depending on the species. The North American 17-year cicadas are the most famous, and the simultaneous emergence of thousands of the bumblebee-sized nymphs from the ground followed by their molt into loudly singing adults unfailingly results in considerable news coverage.

hardens, the insect does not grow any larger until the next molt. Molting is also the time when other parts of the insect's body, such as the head and legs, become larger.

The Role of Hormones

Like many other bodily activities, the onset of ecdysis is controlled by hormones. The brain directly or indirectly signals the release of a range of hormones, including some known as ecdysis-triggering hormones (ETHs), that loosen the old cuticle from the newly developing cuticle underneath and otherwise ready the insect to break free from the old hull. Another chemical, bursicon, helps to harden the new cuticle.

Gradual Development

Some insects develop from egg-hatching to adult by a series of baby steps, growing larger at each step, but changing only minimally in form from the last. Scientists use the term ametabolous (meaning "without metamorphosis") to describe these gradually developing insects. Ametabolous insects include the wingless orders, such as the bristletails, silverfish, and firebrats.

Upon hatching, bristletails, silverfish, and firebrats look like small versions of adults, but without any

external reproductive organs. As they grow from one instar to the next, they become larger and larger, and eventually make the change from larva to adult when they gain their external reproductive organs. Once they are adults, they continue to go through molts. This process is different from that of the winged insects, in which offspring often look quite different from adults, and also gain both reproductive capability as well as their wings only at their last molt. Winged insects never molt again once they become adults. Exceptions to this rule exist. The most notable occurs in the mayflies (order Ephemeroptera) described in an earlier chapter. They are the only winged insects that have one final molt after they get their wings.

Often, grasshoppers change little in appearance from nymph to adult, but the eastern lubber grasshopper (*Romalea microptera*) undergoes a color alteration. The nymph (right) is usually black with one or more yellow stripes. Adults (left) come in different colors, including yellow, tan, and combinations of gray, black, and brown.

Winged Insects

Among most winged insects, larvae and adults are noticeably different. In some species, that disparity is obvious mainly in the wings, which appear only after the final molt when the larvae develop into adults. Otherwise, the larvae look almost identical to the adults. In some instances, especially among those insects that have aquatic larvae and terrestrial adults, the differences between the two life stages are greater. Insects that develop in either of these ways are termed hemimetabolous, which means that they have so-called incomplete metamorphosis. Complete metamorphosis, which is described in the next section, occurs in insects that have an additional pupal stage added to their developmental progress.

When a damselfly or dragonfly transforms from naiad to adult, the exoskeleton splits open down the back of the thorax, and the adult emerges. Known as an exuvia, the spent shell (shown) remains behind.

Slow but Sure

Insects that exhibit incomplete metamorphosis include members of the true bugs (order Hemiptera), the grasshoppers, crickets, and others in the order Orthoptera, the mantids (order Mantodea), cockroaches (order Blattodea), and others. Their larvae, called nymphs, start out with the same basic body shape of the adult, although they may have a different body color or pattern. As time passes, they begin to grow their wings. The typical true bug nymph, for example, develops four tiny wingpads, small flaplike projections that extend from the thorax, by the time it reaches its third instar. Over the next two molts, the wingpads become larger, and although they are still nonfunctional, they begin to take on the look of the adult's wings. At the final developmental molt, the nymph becomes an adult with full-sized, working wings and functional reproductive organs.

One Big Leap

Some hemimetabolous insects proceed through all of their larval stages with only gradual changes in their outward appearance, except the last one. At that stage, the insect undergoes a major shift in body structure and often lifestyle. Dragonflies and damselflies epitomize this form of metamorphosis. Dragonfly and damselfly larvae are aquatic nymphs, or naiads, that breathe through gills. A dragonfly naiad's gills, however, are nowhere near the head, but are located inside the rectum. A damselfly naiad's gills stretch behind its abdomen as three noticeable appendages that look like thin tails. As a naiad is ready to go through its final maturation molt, it crawls from the water onto land. The top of its thorax splits, and an adult begins to emerge. As the pressure from its hemolymph, or "blood," expands its body to its new and larger adult size, the hemolymph also begins pumping into the veins of the wings and unfurling them. Often, hundreds of dragonflies from a single species will go through this process simultaneously, creating several hours of fascinating viewing for observers who are lucky enough to be in the right place at the right time. Humans, however, are not the only animals interested in mass

dragonfly metamorphosis. Birds frequently descend on the insects, which are extremely vulnerable from the time they creep out of the water until their wings fully open and harden, and they are able to fly.

Above: Dragonflies and damselflies (in the order Odonata) make up one of the groups of insects that exhibit metamorphosis described as "incomplete." This means that they develop from egg to larva/nymph/naiad to adult, and lack the pupal stage. Here, a newly emerged adult dragonfly rests above the discarded shell of its naiad stage.

Right: The adult male dobsonfly has a pair of long mandibles that he uses to grasp the female during mating. The female (shown here) has much smaller jaws. Anglers, however, are most familiar with the jaws of dobsonfly larvae, called hellgrammites. Common fish bait, hellgrammites can inflict a painful bite.

LARVAE WITH A BITE

Adult dobsonflies (order Megaloptera) are large-winged insects that lay their eggs near the water. Anglers, however, are often more familiar with their hard-biting larvae, which typically live under rocks in streams. The larvae, called hellgrammites and often reaching 3 or 4 inches (7.6–10.2 cm) in length, have jaws powerful enough to break the skin of a human finger and draw blood, but anglers still tempt fate with the larvae because they are also excellent bait for trout.

Amazing Transformations

Some larvae have no resemblance whatsoever to the adults they will become: grubs do not look like adult beetles, maggots do not share the appearance of flies, and caterpillars have little in common with butterflies. The amazing transformation from a fleshy larva to an adult occurs during the additional phase of the pupa. Insects that go through this process are holometabolous, which means that they undergo "complete" metamorphosis that includes the pupal stage.

What Happens?

In complete metamorphosis, the larva are wormlike, sometimes very soft creatures that grow but otherwise maintain a similar appearance at each molt. As the larvae increase in size, groups of cells called imaginal disks also grow, although they do not develop into any organs until the pupal instar. This stage has various forms. In moths, the pupa are typically enclosed in a silken cocoon, while the pupa of many butterflies may develop inside a hardened chrysalis. Many of these insects pupate above the ground, but others, such as a variety of beetles and the mosquitoes, pupate underground or in the water.

In all cases, the pupal stage is one of great changes. Certain adult organs begin to take shape from similar larval organs, but many of them arise from the imaginal disks, which finally begin to develop into adult tissues, organs, and entire structures, such as the legs, eyes, and wings, during the pupal stage. Once the transformation is complete, the insect emerges in its final, adult form.

Below right: This caterpillar will eventually develop into one of the world's largest moths, the atlas moth (*Attacus atlas*) of Southeast Asia. Adult moths have a wing surface area of 65 square inches (400 sq. cm) or more.

Below: Recently emerged from its chrysalis, this atlas moth will soon be able to fly. Its wings have nearly finished expanding to their full size. The wingspan of an atlas moth can range from 7 to nearly 12 inches (18–30 cm).

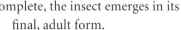

Houseflies

All of the flies (order Diptera) are holometabolous, and the houseflies exhibit the typical method of this group. Eggs hatch into legless larvae, the whitish maggots that generally draw looks of repulsion from humans. Each maggot grows through its instars until it reaches its last larval stage. At this point, its outer skin hardens into a shell, called a puparium, and the larva becomes a pupa. If conditions are right, the pupal transformation may only take a few days, and an adult will break out of the capsulelike puparium.

Mosquitoes

Although they are also in the fly order, mosquitoes develop differently. For one thing, they need water, although they do not need much. A female will lay her eggs in any source of calm

These larvae of the common pest mosquito *Culex pipiens* dangle characteristically underwater. Sticking up from the rear of the abdomen, a breathing tube breaks the water surface so that the larvae can take in air. When they are disturbed, the larvae will squirm deeper into the water and resurface later.

water, including birdbaths, dog dishes, and even puddles left by a shoe print. Within about a week, the eggs hatch into larvae that often dangle just underwater, sometimes breathing with gills and sometimes with an abdominal breathing tube that breaks the surface. The larvae are called wigglers, a term that describes their active gyrations in the water. Most pupae are immobile or nearly so, but not those of the mosquitoes. Mosquito pupae, known as tumblers, can squirm through the water column, a behavior that allows them to reach the water surface and take periodic breaths of air through tubes. The typical mosquito pupal stage lasts about two days, after which a fully functional adult emerges.

ENGINEERING AN ESCAPE

Before it pupates, the larva of the goldenrod elliptical-gall moth prepares its exit hole, although it will not use it for a while yet. It chews through the gall's wall, widening it toward the outside, and from the inside, plugs the hole shut with silk and bits of plant material. By beveling the hole in this way, the insect can push out the plug easily from the inside, but potential predators cannot easily push it in.

CHAPTER 17

SURVIVING FROM YEAR TO YEAR

ROCK CRAWLERS, INSECTS IN THE GENUS *GRYLLOBLATTA*, live high in the mountains of the Pacific Northwest where snow covers the ground much of the year. They continue feeding and moving even when the air outside hovers around the freezing point. When the temperature rises above 65°F (18°C), they become lethargic, and at a few degrees warmer, they begin to die.

Rock crawlers are, of course, exceptions. Temperatures of 65°F or above are typically quite tolerable for the vast majority of insects, while freezing temperatures would immobilize, if not kill, most adults. Yet, insects survive frigid winter seasons. How do they do it? Some insects produce antifreeze that keeps at least the cells in their vital organs from experiencing irreparable damage. Many insects find a protected, relatively warm spot in their habitat and avoid freezing temperatures there, or they migrate out altogether. Some adults, however, are unable to make it through winter alive, and only their eggs or larvae make it to the following spring.

Whatever their survival skills, an insect's life is fleeting. Only a small percentage of all adult insects survive from one year to the next, and for most, their entire adult life span is counted in days.

Left: This bee is gathering nectar, a principal ingredient of honey. Come winter, honey bees will rely on the stores of honey that they produced over the previous year. Inset: For most adult insects, winter weather is fatal. Some, however, such as honey bees, can survive the cold. Entire colonies—adults, pupae, and eggs—survive the winter in their nests or in the man-made hive boxes, as shown here.

Migration

Monarch butterflies are the best-known migrating butterflies in North America, with some traveling from Canada to Mexico. Although most monarchs head south for the winter, some head west instead. The monarchs pictured here are catching some sunshine in an overwintering grove in Santa Cruz, California.

Some insects handle cold winter weather the same way that humans do: they head to an area with a warmer climate, occasionally hundreds and hundreds of miles away. Sometimes, a single individual makes the entire round-trip trek itself, but often the two-way journey is a multigenerational undertaking, and occasionally even the one-way legs of the trip are split into short hops made by successive generations.

The Great Monarch Migration

Perhaps the most amazing of the migratory insects is the monarch butterfly (*Danaus plexippus*). At about 10 miles (16 km) per hour, they are not exceptionally fast fliers, but they are tenacious. A monarch that spends the warm months in Canada or the northeastern United States will embark in late summer on a 2,000-mile (3,219 km) flight south to its wintering ground in certain Mexican mountain forests—the same place where its ancestors spent their winters. The achievement is an astonishing one. The migrating monarchs were all born over the summer and are making the trip for the first time. Scientists are still unsure how the butterflies find their way, but millions make the journey south every year. The butterflies spend the next few months in huge roosts numbering in the millions. During the winter months, the monarchs are inactive, but by spring they are ready to mate and to begin their long flights northward.

The migratory flights are not continuous. Individual butterflies will stop often along the away to feed and to rest. Huge gatherings of monarchs can cover tree branches with their orange wings. At Point Pelee National Park in Ontario, Canada, for example, park officials issue daily monarch reports, and throngs of people visit from late August to early October for a chance at witnessing the spectacle of southbound butterflies. When the butterflies make the trip back north the following spring, only some individuals survive

CLIMATE CHANGE AND MONARCHS

Monarch butterflies from the United States and Canada migrate and roost for the winter in only a few small areas of mountain forest in Mexico. Scientists fear that loss of the forest patches could spell doom for these populations. In 2003, a research group from the University of Minnesota and the University of Kansas completed a computer analysis of the effects of global warming on the forests. The analysis indicated that global warming heightened the probability of increased precipitation, including ice and snow—conditions that would be perilous for the butterflies overwintering there. The research group predicted that the climate changes could appear by the year 2050.

tiny potato leaf hopper (*Empoasca fabae*). One of the smallest known long-distance winter migrators, the green adult hoppers grow only to about an eighth of an inch (0.3 cm) long. Yet, these insects travel from their wintering grounds in the southern United States to points as far north as the Upper Midwest and Canada. They accomplish the feat by flying high enough to tap into the prevailing southerly winds, which carry the insects along. It is not a completely free ride. The hoppers must continue to flap their tiny wings to stay in the wind current. Once the hoppers reach their summer home, the insects multiply profusely and often become pests as they descend on farm fields to feast on potato, bean, strawberry, and other crops.

Above: The monarch butterflies that overwinter in Mexico choose from only a few select spots in mountain forests. Scientists fear that global warming could have an impact on those forests and threaten the butterflies that roost there.

Below: Monarchs are not the only distance migrating insects. This tiny potato leaf hopper (*Empoasca fabae*) is one of the species that makes a long trek. Using wind currents to help them along, some will travel from the Upper Midwest and Canada to the southern United States each year.

the entire trip. Often, they die en route. Since they have already mated and the females have laid eggs, however, their young will continue the trip and eventually arrive at their summer home. Like their parents, these new arrivals will perish before the next fall migration south, and younger generations will carry on the practice.

Beyond Butterflies

Some people may not find it surprising that the relatively large-sized and broad-winged monarchs migrate far and wide, yet surely they are taken aback by the migratory flight of the

Adult Hibernation

In the winter, ladybugs will converge by the hundreds to hibernate. This clump of ladybugs has found a relatively warm and protected spot within the soft folds of a mullein plant at Kaibab Plateau, Arizona.

Because insects are cold-blooded (ectothermic), an individual's body temperature typically mimics the outside temperature year-round. In temperate climates, that means a warm body in the summer and a cold one in the winter. A variety of insects survive the prolonged and potentially fatal frigid weather by entering hibernation diapause, a period marked by slowed body processes, and no or very little activity. As temperatures warm, their internal workings begin to rev up, the insects start to move again, and soon they are ready to go back to their normal lives.

Antifreeze

For many insects, an extra ingredient is the key to their overwintering strategy. Just as a person adds antifreeze to a car to keep it running in cold weather, an insect produces one of several chemicals or proteins to help at least the vital organs resist freezing solid, and to keep the insect alive until spring. One of the compounds is called ethylene glycol and is the same chemical used in many automobile antifreeze mixtures. Scientists have recently also identified a number of insect antifreeze proteins that appear to prevent damaging ice crystals from growing in the six-legged creatures' bodies. Insects at many stages use the antifreeze chemicals or proteins, usually in concert with their entrance into hibernation diapause. The combination is often a life-saving one.

Ladybugs

Ladybugs are some of the best known among the insect hibernators. A person removing a piece of siding from a house in a winter month may find hundreds of the insects all tucked together in a clump. They also hibernate under pieces of loose bark or beneath piles of

dead leaves. Although they may look dead, most of them probably are not. Come the first days of spring, they will begin to crawl slowly from their winter refuge. Occasionally, even a few warm January or February days will be enough to entice some ladybugs to go exploring, and these sometimes find small openings in a wall or a crack around a window and enter the relative warmth of the house.

Mourning Cloak

The mourning cloak (*Nymphalis antiopa*) is distinctive with its purplish brown wings colored with a line of blue dots and edged in cream. A North American and Eurasian species, it is also known for being one of the few butterflies that survive the cold winter months as adults. The butterflies find a slot under the loose bark or in a crevice of a tree and slide inside. When early spring arrives, they emerge and are often the only adult butterflies for miles. They mate and the females

lay a brood of eggs, often on a willow stem. This will be the only generation for the year. The eggs hatch into spiny, red-spotted, black-and-gray caterpillars. The caterpillars stay together as they grow but eventually move apart to pupate. The pupal stage lasts about three weeks, and when the adults emerge, they commence feeding to build up fat reserves in preparation for their winter hibernation diapause.

This lovely mourning cloak is one of the few butterflies that can tolerate cold weather as adults. In the very early spring when temperatures are still winterlike, they are the first of the adult butterflies to flutter about.

INSECT RIP VAN WINKLE

Diapause does not only occur during the winter. When an insect is faced with extreme conditions, including drought or excessive heat, many will suspend their development until circumstances improve. Some can remain in diapause for years. The yucca moth *Prodoxus y-inversus* is an example. Members of this species may spend 16 to 17 years as pupae before finally emerging from their cocoons. The adults are colored in brown and cream and have a wingspan of 0.4 to 0.6 inches (1–1.5 cm).

Overwintering

For a great many insects, adults live only long enough to mate before dying, and those that live longer cannot survive prolonged, cold temperatures common to winters in temperate or colder climates. These species persist from year to year, however, because the eggs, larvae, or pupae can withstand the frigid season to develop in the coming, warmer months. Examples of all three follow.

Above: To the irritation of many gardeners, Japanese beetles cause damage in both their larval and adult stages. The adults, shown here eating rose leaves, will eat everything but the leaf veins. Larvae, which spend the winter underground, come to the surface in the spring with a hearty appetite.

Right: For many insects, only the eggs can survive cold winters. Gypsy moths, for instance, overwinter as eggs that look like slightly bumpy, white or tan patches on tree trunks. In the spring, the eggs hatch into red- and blue-spotted caterpillars. In numbers, the caterpillars feed heavily on oak, maple, and other tree vegetation.

Overwintering as Eggs

Considered a serious threat to hardwood trees in parts of the United States, the gypsy moth (*Lymantria dispar*) is one of the insects that overwinters in the egg stage. None of its other life stages—larva, pupa, or adult—survive the winter season. Although the gypsy egg masses are often readily visible on tree trunks and branches, people frequently overlook the tan to whitish patches. Many organizations have mounted publicity campaigns to educate people about the appearance of the eggs, because the transport of infested firewood is believed to be one of the primary ways that the moths spread to new locations.

Overwintering as Larvae

Almost anyone who has shoveled a hole in good soil or under the lawn in the fall is familiar with Japanese beetle (*Popillia japonica*) larvae, or grubs, that are preparing to overwinter. The adult is an oval, shiny green and copper beetle about 0.3 to 0.4 inches (0.8–1.1 cm) long. The grub is soft, and white, with six obvious legs just behind the head. It is larger than the adult and can reach 1.3 inches (3.2 cm) in length, although its size is somewhat concealed because the grubs quickly curl into a C shape when uncovered. The beetle's life cycle is an annual one, with each adult female typically laying three to five dozen eggs during the mid- to late-summer. The

eggs hatch into grubs, which feed and grow to their third instar by the time they are ready to enter hibernation diapause. At this stage, the grubs dig deep into the ground and spend the winter there. In the spring, they tunnel back to the surface to do more feeding and developing before pupating and emerging as adults by midsummer.

Like gypsy moths, Japanese beetles are considered pest species. The larvae cause damage to plants by munching on roots, and the adult beetles are notorious for skeletonizing, or devouring everything but the veins, of a wide variety of plant leaves. They also consume flowers. Native to Japan, the beetles were introduced to North America by at least 1916 and now have spread to much of the eastern and central United States and parts of Canada.

HONEY BEES VERSUS BUMBLEBEES

Honey bees and bumblebees overwinter in different ways. In honey bees, the entire colony survives inside the nest and feeds on the honey it has stored over the previous year. Bumblebees do not overwinter as a colony and have no need to produce as much honey. In the fall, young queens leave their home nests, mate, and each finds a protected spot to spend the cold months. When the weather finally warms, the fertile females start new colonies.

Overwintering as Pupae

The spiny oakworm moth (*Anisota stigma*) spends its cold winters as a pupa. The adult moth, which lives mainly in the eastern United States, is orange- to yellow-tinged tan in color with a small white spot on each forewing. Females lay their eggs in midsummer on leaves, and the eggs hatch and grow into mainly orange-pink to orange-brown caterpillars covered with black spines. The caterpillars favor a diet of oak leaves, and continue feeding until the fall when they burrow a few inches into the ground and pupate. The insect remains in the pupal stage until the following summer, when it finally metamorphoses into an adult to repeat the life cycle.

Adult spiny oakworm moths lay their eggs in the summer, and the dark-headed larvae (shown here) have plenty of time to feed and grow before pupating later in the year. They spend the winter and spring as pupae, emerging the following summer as adults.

Life Span

Right: Laboratory fruit flies are a favorite subject for scientists conducting genetic studies. In one set of experiments, scientists identified genetic mutations that serve to double the fly's life span.

Below: Depending on the species, some cicadas live a decade or more. They spend almost their entire lives underground as nymphs, and then emerge for a brief time as a winged adult (left). The discarded hull of a nymph is at right.

For humans, the adult stage of life is usually the longest. For insects, however, the adult stage is one of the shortest. In fact, some insects have only a week and sometimes less to carry out all of their adult duties. Fortunately, their to-do list often has only one item: reproduce. A few insects have extended adult phases. These include the queens of ant colonies. In some zoos that have kept colonies for a decade or more, a single queen ant can continue to rule the nest as long as it exists. Her longevity does not extend to her offspring, however. The typical worker ant lives less than a year, and sometimes only a few months.

Fruit Flies

Scientists frequently turn to fruit flies of one type, *Drosophila melanogaster,* for their studies. They do this in part because of the insects' short life spans. Since a fruit fly's entire lifetime occurs over a period of about a month when they are kept at a balmy 84°F (29°C), a researcher can run experiments on several different

generations in a year's time. A number of these experiments actually center on the fruit fly's life span itself. In some, researchers have teased out which genes help certain fruit flies live longer. For example, researchers at the University of Connecticut Health Center identified mutations in a gene that allow a fruit fly to live twice the normal length. They named the gene Indy, short for "I'm not dead yet," a line from the 1975 film *Monty Python and the Holy Grail.*

Ripe Old Age

One of the insects with an extremely long life span is the periodical, or 17-year, cicada. These insects spend nearly all of their 17 years as nymphs that live

"The butterfly counts not months but moments, and has time enough."

—RABINDRANATH TAGORE

underground. Other cicada species share the extended nymphal stage but do not live quite as long. Some of these have life spans of 6 to 13 years.

Besides the cicadas, many of the dragonflies and damselflies have a prolonged life, much of it spent as an aquatic nymph, or naiad. Some naiads may survive in the water for one to six years before finally creeping onto the shore to metamorphose into adults. A few species even survive the winter as adults by migrating. One is the variegated meadowhawk (*Sympetrum corruptum*), a clear-winged, yellow or reddish dragonfly with a body 1.5 to 2 inches (3.8–5.1 cm) long. Adults migrate from the northwestern United States to warmer spots south. Efforts are now under way to learn more about their migration route and life history.

Mysteries Abound

For many insects, however, scientists do not know how long they live, or for that matter, how they spend their lives. It is not that the species are extremely secretive (although some of them surely are), or that they live in especially hard-to-reach locations (although some of them do). The challenge arises from their sheer number. With hundreds of thousands of species on Earth, many of them still to be discovered, mysteries will remain for many, many years to come.

Some dragonflies migrate to a warmer climate for the winter. Scientists are currently trying to learn exactly where the variegated meadowhawk goes when it leaves its summer home in the northwestern United States.

Glossary

AEDEAGUS. The male insect's reproductive structure, which has a similar function to the mammalian penis.

APOSEMATIC COLORATION. A conspicuous color of an organism that has the effect of warding off other animals. It is fairly common among insects that are distasteful or poisonous to potential predators.

Junonia coenia, or the common buckeye butterfly.

BIOINDICATOR. An organism that can be used to determine the health of an ecosystem. An organism's density, for example, may serve as an indication of pollution level.

CASTE. A specialized position in a society. Among insects, castes are common in highly social species, such as many bees, wasps, and ants, and may include such positions as reproductive male or female, worker, or soldier.

CAUDAL FILAMENT. A thin extension beyond the abdomen. It is present in some insects, including certain mayflies (order Ephemeroptera), which have caudal filaments that appear between two long cerci.

CERCI. Appendages commonly extending from the tip of the abdomen in many insects, and having the function of rear feelers. Typically, insects with cerci have two of these appendages.

CLOSED CIRCULATORY SYSTEM. A cardiovascular system in which the blood is contained within vessels and does not directly bathe the bodily tissues. All vertebrates and some invertebrates, although not insects, have a closed circulatory system.

COEVOLUTION. The evolution of separate species that occurs as a result of the ecological interaction between them. In other words, evolutionary changes in one species spur changes in the other, which in turn incite further changes in the first, and so on, so that the evolution of each occurs in tandem with the other.

COLD-BLOODEDNESS. Condition in which an organism's body temperature changes with the ambient temperature. This is also known as ectothermy.

COMPLETE METAMORPHOSIS. A form of insect development, it includes four stages: egg, larva, pupa, and adult.

COMPOUND EYE. An eye composed of several to many individual eye units, which are called ommatidia. Insects typically have two compound eyes, as well as a number of simple eyes, which are called ocelli.

CUTICLE. The outer surface of an insect's body.

ECDYSIS. The shedding of the outer skin layer, which in insects is the cuticle.

ELYTRA. The leathery, frequently stiff, forewings in beetles and other insects. The elytra, also sometimes called wing covers, often conceal the membranous hind wings that are folded beneath when the insect is at rest. During flight, the hind wings unfurl and provide the flight function.

EUSOCIAL BEHAVIOR. The highest level of social behavior among the insects. Eusocial insects live and work together with other members of their species, distributing labor to different castes and exhibiting cooperative care of the brood by society members other than the birth parents. Such societies frequently have few reproductive individuals, while the remaining are sterile.

EXOSKELETON. The hardened outer structure, or "shell," of an insect and some other invertebrates. Muscles attach to the inner surface of the exoskeleton.

FRASS. The feces of insect larvae.

GALL. An abnormal tissue outgrowth found on plants, often on the leaves or stems of wildflowers, shrubs, and trees. Insect infestation is one cause of galls. The size, shape, and site of the gall is often useful in identifying the associated insect.

HEMELYTRA. The half-hardened, half-membranous forewings seen in many insects in the order Hemiptera (the true bugs). When the insect is at rest, the forewings are held so that the membranous portions, which are toward the rear of the wings, overlap.

HEMOLYMPH. An insect's "blood," although it does not contain hemoglobin nor does it carry oxygen, as human blood does. An insect's hemolymph does share many of the jobs of human blood, such as transporting nutrients and waste products.

INCOMPLETE METAMORPHOSIS. A form of development in some insects, it includes three stages: egg, nymph (or naiad), and adult.

INSTAR. The stage in an insect's development that occurs between molts. Larval insects may progress through several instars before becoming an adult.

NAIAD. An aquatic nymph.

Various females of the Scarabaeidae family of beetles show off their metallic coloring.

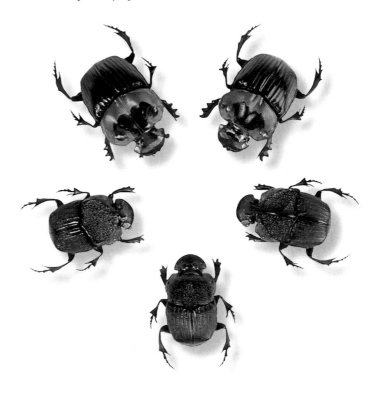

NYMPH. The immature form of an insect that goes through incomplete metamorphosis. Nymphs generally look much like the adults but lack functioning wings and reproductive organs.

OCELLI. Simple eyes that register the presence or absence of light. Common to most insects, they typically accompany two compound eyes, which provide visual detail.

OMMATIDIUM. An individual unit in a compound eye. Like the human eye, it includes a cornea, lens, and a cluster of photoreceptors.

OVIPOSITOR. An elongate, egg-laying structure seen in many female insects and used to place eggs in vegetation, rotting wood, or other locations. In some insects, such as female bees and wasps, the ovipositor is modified into a stinger.

OPEN CIRCULATORY SYSTEM. A cardio-vascular system in which the blood, or hemolymph in the case of insects, directly bathes tissues and organs within the body. All insects and some other invertebrates have an open circulatory system.

PARTHENOGENESIS. A form of reproduction in which the female lays unfertilized, but viable eggs that develop into functional offspring. It is common among many insects.

PHEROMONE. A chemical, released by an organism, that conveys information to other organisms. Pheromones primarily assist communication among members of the same species, but they are sometimes useful to other animals, such as predators that follow pheromones to prey.

PRONOTUM. The first portion of an insect's thorax. In many insects, it is greatly enlarged to cover much of the insect's head and sometimes also extends over the abdomen.

PUPA. The developmental phase between larva and adult in insects that undergo complete metamorphosis. A typical pupa is surrounded by a hardened case or a silken cocoon, and is outwardly inactive.

SEXUAL DIMORPHISM. A noticeable physical difference between genders of the same species.

SPERMATHECA. A sperm-storing sac associated with the reproductive tract of many female insects that are able to delay fertilization of their eggs until some time after copulation.

SPERMATOPHORE. A sperm packet produced by many male insects.

Moths come in many variations, as this array of hawkmoths demonstrates.

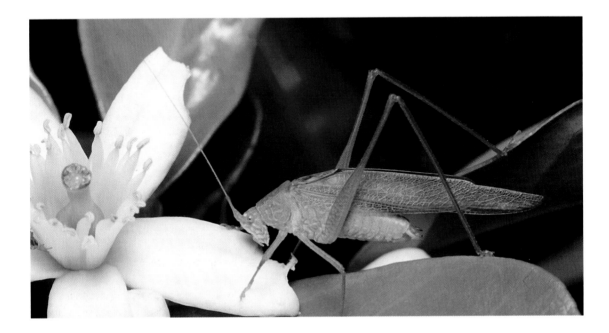

SPIRACLES. External openings of an insect's respiratory system. They open along either side of the thorax and abdomen to allow oxygen to enter an internal network of interconnecting tubes where it is distributed to tissues and organs. The spiracles also allow carbon dioxide to exit.

SUBSOCIAL BEHAVIOR. A level of social behavior among insects in which members of a species live together at least temporarily in small, usually family groups, and exhibit some type of brood care, such as feeding the young or protecting them from potential predators.

SUBSPECIES. A subdivision of a species. Subspecies typically live in geographically distinct areas and have distinct physical features.

TEGMINA. The leathery forewings of grasshoppers, crickets, katydids, cockroaches, mantids, and other insects. Tegmina cover a second pair of flight wings, the hind wings, which are larger and membranous. They are sometimes called elytra, although this term is often reserved for beetles.

TYMBAL. A drumlike membrane occurring on some insects, such as cicadas, and used in the production of sound.

TYMPANA. External ear drums. Depending on the type of insect, the tympana may be located on various parts of the body, including the front legs and the abdomen, or they may be absent.

The green color of this grasshopper affords it protective camouflage from would-be predators.

Find Out More

Its ability to turn its head lends the praying mantid a humanlike aspect.

BOOKS

Adams, Jean, ed. *Insect Potpourri: Adventures in Entomology.* Delray Beach, FL: St. Lucie Press, 1992.

Bates, Marston. *The Natural History of Mosquitoes.* New York: Macmillan, 1949.

Berenbaum, May. *Bugs in the System.* New York: Addison-Wesley, 1995.

——. *Ninety-Nine Gnats, Nits, and Nibblers.* Urbana: University of Illinois-Urbana Press, 1989.

——. *Ninety-Nine More Maggots, Mites, and Munchers.* Urbana: University of Illinois-Urbana Press, 1993.

Carson, Rachel. *Silent Spring.* Boston: Houghton Mifflin, 1962.

Dethier, Vincent G. *To Know a Fly.* San Francisco: Holden-Day, 1962.

——. *The World of the Tent-Makers.* New York: University of Massachusetts Press, 1980.

——. *Crickets and Katydids, Concerts and Solos.* Cambridge, MA: Harvard University Press, 1992.

Dunkle, Sidney W. *Dragonflies through Binoculars: A Guide to Dragonflies of North America.* Oxford, UK: Oxford University Press, 2000.

Eisner, Thomas. *For Love of Insects.* Cambridge, MA: Belknap Press, 2005.

Evans, Howard Ensign. *Life on a Little-Known Planet.* New York: Dell Publishing, 1966.

——. *The Pleasures of Entomology.* Washington, DC: Smithsonian Institution Press, 1985.

——. *Wasp Farm.* Ithaca, NY: Cornell University Press, 1963.

Fitzhugh, Bill. *Pest Control.* New York: Avon Books, 1997.

Frost, S. W. *Insect Life and Insect Natural History.* (Dover reprint). New York: Dover, 1959.

Gibb, T. J. & Oseto, C. Y. *Arthropod Collection and Identification.* New York: Academic Press, 2006.

Goff, M. Lee. *A Fly for the Prosecution: How Insect Evidence Helps Solve Crimes.* Cambridge, MA: Harvard University Press, 2001.

Gordon, David George. *The Compleat Cockroach.* New York: Ten Speed Press, 1996.

Grimaldi, David, and Michael S. Engel. *Evolution of the Insects.* Cambridge, UK: Cambridge University Press, 2005.

Grissell, E. E. *Insects and Gardens.* Portland, OR: Timber Press, 2001.

Grzimek, Bernhard, Neil Schlager, Donna Olendorf, and Melissa C. McDade. *Grzimek's Animal Life Encyclopedia*, Volume 2: *Insects.* Detroit: Thomson Gale, 2003.

Heinrich, Bernd. *Bumblebee Economics.* Cambridge, MA: Harvard University Press, 1979.

——. *In a Patch of Fireweed.* Cambridge, MA: Harvard University Press, 1984.

Holldobler, Bert, and Edward O. Wilson. *Journey to the Ants.* New York: Belknap Press, 1994.

Hubbell, Sue. *A Country Year.* New York: Random House, 1986.

Imes, Rick. *The Practical Entomologist.* New York: Simon & Schuster, 1992.

Johnson, Norman F., and Charles A. Triplehorn. *Borror and DeLong's Introduction to the Study of Insects*. Seventh edition. Belmont, CA: Thomson Brooks/Cole, 2004.

Maeterlinck, Maurice. *The Life of the Bee*. New York: Dodd-Mead, 1914.

Marshall, Stephen A. *Insects: Their Natural History and Diversity: With a Photographic Guide to Insects of Eastern North America*. Richmond Hill, ON: Firefly Books, 2006.

Mound, Laurence. *Insect* (An Eyewitness Guide). London: Dorling Kindersley, 1997.

National Audubon Society. *National Audubon Society Field Guide to North American Butterflies*. New York: Knopf-Chanticleer Press Edition, 1981.

Paulos, Martha, ed. *Insect Asides: Great Poets on Man's Pest Friend*. New York: Viking Studio Books, 1995.

Paulson, Gregory S., Roger D. Akre, and E. Paul Catts. *Insects Did It First*. Fairfield, WA: Ye Galleon Press: 1992.

Silsby, Jill, and Michael J. Parr. *Dragonflies of the World*. Washington, DC: Smithsonian Institution Press, 2001.

Teale, Edwin Way. *The Insect World of J. Henri Fabre*. New York: Harper & Row, 1949.

Tinbergen, Niko. *Curious Naturalists*. Garden City, New York: Doubleday, 1958.

Waldbauer, Gilbert. *What Good Are Bugs? Insects in the Web of Life*. Cambridge, MA: Harvard University Press, 2003.

———. *Millions of Monarchs, Bunches of Beetles: How Insects Find Strength in Numbers*. Cambridge, MA: Harvard University Press, 2001 (reprint).

WEB SITES

DISCOVER ENTOMOLOGY/TEXAS A&M UNIVERSITY
insects.tamu.edu/websites
Links to various insect-related Web sites.

HEXAPODA
tolweb.org/Hexapoda/2528
A comprehensive site covering characteristics of various orders and extensive book, article, and Web site references.

INSECT ORDERS AND COMMON FAMILIES
eny3005.ifas.ufl.edu/lab1/
Reference source with wide-ranging links.

IOWA STATE UNIVERSITY ENTOMOLOGY IMAGE GALLERY
www.ent.iastate.edu/imagegallery/
A substantial photographic collection of insect (and other arthropod) life stages, the plant damage they cause, and links to additional information.

UF BOOK OF INSECT RECORDS
ufbir.ifas.ufl.edu/
An anthology of contributed chapters, a large number from graduate students, that nominate insect species for record-holding characteristics or abilities. It is edited by Thomas J. Walker of the University of Florida Department of Entomology and Nematology.

VERY COOL BUGS
www.insects.org/entophiles/index.html
A compilation of beautiful insect photos accompanying ecological facts, and tips for photographing insects.

Caterpillars come in all colors, from bold multicolored stripes to grassy green solids that camouflage them in leafy environments.

At the Smithsonian

The Smithsonian Institution's National Museum of Natural History is widely regarded as one of the most impressive natural history museums in the world. It is no wonder then that the museum is also home to a highly regarded insect collection.

The O. Orkin Insect Zoo

In 1993, the O. Orkin Insect Zoo opened at the NMNH. For 13 years, it has been one of the Smithsonian's more popular exhibits and has served to educate the public about the incredible and exciting world of insects. The Insect Zoo is home to more than 300 individual live insect and arachnid species, including leaf-cutter ants, walkingsticks, and diving beetles. The insects in the collection all live in meticulously reproduced imitations of their natural habitats, including deserts, tropical rain forests, and even bee trees. By preserving the natural habitats of

The National Museum of Natural History houses an impressive collection of insects at the O. Orkin Insect Zoo.

these organisms, Smithsonian scientists have created a rare museum exhibit that allows visitors to better understand the relationship between a species and their surroundings.

In addition to the impressive diversity of insects on display, the O. Orkin Insect Zoo is also a hands-on learning center. Visitors are actually able to handle live insects and arachnids and even participate in a tarantula feeding. Other features of the zoo are a giant-sized termite mound and the popular interactive display called Our House, Their House. By pushing buttons in front of a three-dimensional model home, visitors can illuminate all the different areas that are host to common household insects such as fleas, cockroaches, and silverfish.

Virtual Tour

If you cannot make it to Washington, D.C., to see the exhibit in person, you can access a virtual zoo tour online at http://www.mnh.si.edu/museum/VirtualTour/Tour/Second/InsectZoo/index.html. The virtual tour contains photographs of many of the zoo's species, as well as the attractions that make the exhibit unique. The Insect Zoo also has a traveling exhibit that brings the insects of the zoo to classrooms and museums all over the United States, promoting insect education.

The Butterfly Habitat Garden

In 1995, the Smithsonian became home to another unique attraction, the Butterfly Habitat Garden. Located between the museums grounds and Washington's Ninth Street tunnel, the Butterfly Habitat Garden is composed of 100 nectar plants that attract a wide variety of butterflies from all over the District of Columbia. The garden, which is divided into

Above and left: Plants or insects? Both on-site and online, the Insect Zoo offers visitors information on the protective camouflage used by various insects, such as these leafy walking sticks.

A variety of local butterflies, such as this yellow sulphur (above) and the red admiral (below) can be viewed at the Smithsonian's Butterfly Habitat Garden in Washington, D.C.

four different "habitats" (Meadow, Woods Edge, Urban Garden, and Wetland), has been home to more than 30 species of butterfly. In 2007, the museum plans to open an indoor butterfly exhibit called Butterflies and Plants: Partners in Evolution. This exhibit will also feature live butterflies and plants and focus on the relationship between butterflies and their environment.

The National Insect Collection

All of the insects that appear in the exhibits at the Insect Zoo and the Butterfly Habitat Garden are part of the National Insect Collection. The National Insect Collection is composed of more than 35 million specimens from all over the globe. The collection is maintained by etymologists from three different organizations: the Smithsonian Institution Department of Entomology, the Systematic Entomology Laboratory of USDA, and the Walter Reed Army Institute of Research Biosystematics Unit.

Information and Hours

The National Museum of Natural History is located on Tenth Street and Constitution Avenue NW in Washington, D.C., and is open seven days a week from 10 AM to 5:30 PM. Admission is free. For more information about any of the Smithsonian Institution's museums, galleries, programs, and exhibits send an e-mail to info@si.edu or call (202) 633-1000.

A glimpse at the vast resources of the National Insect Collection.

Index

Acknowledgments and Credits

The author would like to acknowledge those associated with the Fish Lake Biological Program and with field-biology programs everywhere. Their students become the future stewards of our wild and wonderful planet. And I dedicate this book to my husband Steve Zaglaniczny, who listens patiently while I tell—and retell—countless tales from my adventures outdoors.

The author and publisher also offer thanks to those closely involved in the creation of this volume: Gary F. Hevel, Department of Entomology, National Museum of Natural History; Ellen Nanney, Senior Brand Manager, Katie Mann, and Carolyn Gleason with Smithsonian Business Ventures; Collins Reference executive editor Donna Sanzone, editor Lisa Hacken, and editorial assistant Stephanie Meyers; consultant Catherine N. Duckett; Hydra Publishing president Sean Moore, publishing director Karen Prince, senior editor/designer Lisa Purcell, art director Brian MacMullen, designer Erika Lubowicki, production editor Eunho Lee, editorial director Aaron Murray, picture researcher Ben DeWalt, editors Marjorie Galen, Michael Smith, Suzanne Lander, Andy Lawler, and Rachael Lanicci, proofreader Glenn Novak, and indexer Amber Rose.

CREDITS

The following abbreviations are used: JI—© 2007 Jupiterimages Corporatin; PR—Photo Researchers, Inc.; SPL—Science Photo Library; FI—FI; iSP—© iStockPhoto.com; SS—ShutterStock; IO—Index Open; BS—Big Stock Photo; WK—Wikimedia; LoC—Library of Congress; NPS—National Park Service

(t=top; b=bottom; l=left; r=right; c=center)

What Is an Insect?
iii iSP/Alexander Omelko ivbg SS/Dainis Derics vi SS/Yaroslav 1 JI 2 JI 3tl JI 3br JI

Chapter 1: Natural Beauties
4bg SS/Eric Lawton 6bg JI 6tl JI 8 SS/Luis César Tejo 9cl SS/Keith Allen Hughes 9br JI 10cl NPS/Richard Lake 10br SS/Travis Klein 11tr JI 11br JI 12 iSP/lauriek 13t SS/Tim Zurowski 13bl Adrian Fowles 14cl iSP/Alex Omelko 14b JI 15t JI 15br JI 16t JI 16c JI 16c JI 16br SS/Lincoln Rogers 16bg JI 17t JI 17cl JI 17tr WK 17br Clipart.com

Chapter 2: Just Bizarre
18bg SS/Jan Erasmus 18tr JI 20 WK/Klaus Gebhart 20bg SS/Graham Prentice 21 Dana Rose/insectimages.org 22 JI 23 WK/Hauke Koch 24tl JI 24br Leah Descamps 25 PR/Gary Retherford 26cl LoC 26br JI 27 iSP/tacojim 28tr JI 28bl JI 28bg JI 29br JI 29tl Dr. Steve Taylor

Chapter 3: A Closer View
30bg SS/Kinlem 30tr Jason J. Jusveth 32 SS/Mike Pluth 33b /photobar 33tr SS/Steve McWilliam 34 JI 35 PR/Volker Steger 36l WK/Sanjay Acharya 36tr JI 37 Matt Yoder/ Texas A&M University 38 PR/Kenneth H. Thomas 39tl WK 39br FI/James B. Hanson 40tl Terry Langhorn 40br Ken Crossland 41 FI/Steven Katovich

Chapter 4: Spectacular Camouflage
42 SS/Jonathan Oldham 44bg PR/Dr. Paul A. Zahl

44tl WK/Fir002 46bl JI 46tr PR/Richard R. Hansen 47 iSP/Ra'id Khalil 48 PR/Francesco Tomasinell 49 WK SS/Ra'id Khalil 50bg SS/Carlos S. Santa Maria 51tr JI 51br SS/Tyler Fox 52cl LoC 52bl WK/Olaf Leillinger 53 WK/Olaf Leillinger

Chapter 5: Mistaken Identity
54bg BS/Valery Kirsanov 54tl SS/Coverstock 56bl SS/Patrick Lamont 56br WK 57tr SS/R. Gino Santa Maria 57b Bugguide.net/Tom Bently 58bl SS/Gertjan Hooijer 58tr SS/Alexsander Isachenko 59br WK 59cl SS/Cre8tive Images 60 iSP/Michael Pettigrew 61t PR/Dr. John Brackenbury 61b Bugguide.net/Tony DiTerlizzi

Chapter 6: Active Defense
62bg SS/Michael DeGasperis 62tr iSP/Craig Foster 64 National Biological Information Infrastructure/Thomas Hermann/Public Domain 65tl SS/Fotosav 65br PR/James H. Robinson 66 JI 67bl PR/Eye of Science 67tr SS/Andriy Rovenko 68cl SS/Lee and Marleigh Freyenhagen 68br SS/Eric Isselée 69 SS/Dave Evangelista 70cl WK 70br WK 71br Morgue File/Calgrin 71bg SS/Tim Zurowski

Chapter 7: On the Attack
72bg SS/Rodney Mehring 72tr SS/Yaroslav 74 SS/James Phelps Jr. 75tr SS/Rodney Mehring 75bl iSP/Marissa Childs 76 FI/Daniel Wojcik 77 PR/Sinclair Stammers 78 WK 79 WK/Orchi 80 SS/Alle 81 WK

Chapter 8: Getting Around
82bg SS/Pixelman 84bg SS/Giuseppe Nocera 84tl SS/Joanna Zopoth-Lipiejko 86 WK 87tr WK 87br WK 88tl SS/Romanchuck Dimitry 88bl WK/Shiva Shankar 89 SS/Cre8tive Images 90bl WK/Sebastian Stabinger 90br SS/Sergey Petrov 91tr iSP/Jeridu 91bl iSP/Felix Mockel 92 iSP/Eris Forehand 93tr SS/Steve Shoup 93br BS/Pavel Lebedinsky

Chapter 9: What's on the Menu
94tl SS/Dusan Dobes 94bg SS/Stephen Bonk 96tl SS/Ryan Morgan 96br SS/Rose 97 SS/Irving Lu 98 WK/Philipp Weigell 99c WK 99br PR/Larry West 100tl iSP/Ryan Poling 100bl BS/Amalea 101tr JI 101bl JI 101bg JI 102tl SS/Hway Kiong Lim 102br SS/David Pinn 103 SS/Tim Zurowski 104bl SS/Justin Hourigan 104br BS/Jacom Stephens 105 PR/Gregory D. Dimijian, M.D. 106t PR/Gianni Tortoli 106bl WK 107 WK

Chapter 10: Creature Comforts
108bg PR/A. Cosmos Blank 108tr iSP/Rainer Hillebrand 110tr SS/David Davis 110bl WK 111cr iSP/Jorge Delgado 111bg BS/Howard Cheek 112br IO/Photos.com Select 112bl BS/Sara Otto 113tr JI 113br SS/Matka Wariatka 114 WK/Fir002 115tl WK/Armon 115br WK 116t BS/Christopher Waters 116b BS/Pat Edens 116bg JI 117 SS/Emilia Kun 118tl SS/Stuart Elflett 118br SS/Thomas Mounsey 119 BS/Bent Nordeng

Chapter 11: Insect Communication
120tl SS/ Frank Boellmann 120bg iSP/Hung Meng Tan 122 iSP/Laurie Knight 123br BS/Vladimir Ivanov 123cr Bugguide.net/Craig Biegler 124tl PR/Sinclair Stammers 124t SS/Koval 125 SS/Steve McWilliam 126tl WK 126t SS/Ra'id Khalil 127 iSP/Steve Geer 128 PR/Lena Untidt/Bonnier Publications 129tr Science Photo Library 129br JI

Chapter 12: Six-Legged Society
130bg SS/Steve Cukrov 130tr BS/Irina Tischenko 132 USDA 132b USDA/Scott Bauer 132tr iSP/Norman Reid 133cl USDA 134t SS/Dragan Trifunovic 134bg JI 135tl PR/Scott Camazine 135cr BS/Lloyd Paulson 136 SPL/George Bernard 137tr SS/Tim Zurowski 137br SS/Timothy R. Nichols 138 BS/Marek Kosmal 139 WK

Chapter 13: Courting Behavior
140 SS/Inta Eihmane 142bg PR/Gregory K. Scott 142tl Wikipedia/Iron Chris 144 PR/Stuart Wilson 145tl iSP/James Metcalf 145br BS/Barbara Scott 146cl iSP/Kristin Rueber 146br WK/Andre Karwath 147 BS/John Lee York 148 WK/Andre Karwath 149tl FI/Whitney Cranshaw 149br USDA Forest Service Archives/Gerald J. Lenhard 150 SS/Sharon D 151tr iSP/proxyminder 151br WK/Mathie Joron 152 SS/Steve Shoup 153 FI/David Jones/University of Georgia 154 SS/Eva Madrazo 155tl SS/Ismael Montero Verdu 155br WK

Chapter 14: Insect Mating
156bg BS/Jasenka Lukša 156tl SS/Tim Zurowski 158 SPL/Dr. George Beccaloni 159 NPS 160 PR/Andrew Syred 161 WK/Rob Knell 162 iSP/Kathy Hicks 163tr PR/Dr. Morley Read 163bl USDS/NPS/Tom Pittenger 164rt WK 164bl PR/Andrew Syred, Sheffield University 165 BS/Scott Impink 166 iSP/Douglas Stener 167t WK 167b JI 168l WK/Luc Viatour 168br iSP/Paul Whillock 169 iSP/Paul Whillock 170tr WK/Andrew Scholbrock 170bl iSP/Judy Worley 171 SS/Alle

Chapter 15: Egg Laying
172bg BS 172tl iSP 174 JI 175tl iSP/Choicegraphx 175tr BS/Jip Fens 176 PR/A. Cosmos Blank 177bl SS/Paulo Neres 177tr North Carolina Cooperative Extension/Debbie Roos 178tr BS/David Acosta Allely 178bl WK/Public Domain 179tr iSP/Jeridu 179bl PR/Peter Chadwick 180 SPL/Adrian Bicker 181tr iSP/Jeridu 181br iSP/Armando Frazao 182 iSP/Susanne Mnich 183 Daniel Mosquin

Chapter 16: Insect Development
184tl SS/Cathy Keifer 184bg BS/Cathy Keifer 186tl Clemson University/USDA/FI 186b BS/Wayne McKown 187 PR/James H. Robinson 188 iSP/Philp Puleo 189tr iSP/Ruta Saulyte-Laurinaviciene 189b USDS/Whitney Cranshaw 190 BS/Martin Vrlik 190bl iSP/Graham Heywood 191br PR/Martin Dohrn

Chapter 17: Surviving from Year to Year
192tr SS/Dusan Po 192bg iSP/Arnstein Berg 194 iSP/Simon Phipps 195tl JI 195br Steve L. Brown/USDA/FI 196 PR/Stuart Wilson 197 BS/Claire Dassy 198tl iSP/Katie Hilbert 198br JI 199 USDA/Lacy L. Hych/FI 200tl JI 200tr iSP/Sergiy Schcherbakov 201 SS/Tim Zurowski

Glossary/Find Out More
202 JI 203 JI 204 JI 205 JI 206 SS 207 IO

At the Smithsonian
208 iSP/Vladimir Ivanov 209t JI 209b JI 210tr JI 210bl JI 211 Smithsonian Institution

Cover Art
Front iSP/Alexander Omelko Back SS/Coko

BOCA RATON PUBLIC LIBRARY, FLORIDA

3 3656 0537795 0

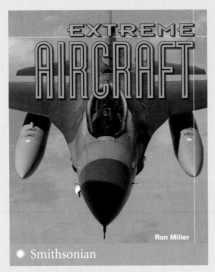

EXTREME AIRCRAFT

Ron Miller

✷ Smithsonian

ISBN 978-0-06-089141-1 (pb)

EXTREME BUGS

Leslie Mertz

✷ Smithsonian

ISBN 978-0-06-089147-3 (pb)

595.7 Mer
Mertz, Leslie A.
Extreme bugs /

GET EXTREME!

The biggest, ...ple extreme
wonders on the ... ...nd explained!

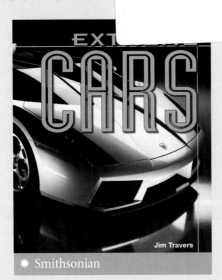

EXTREME CARS

Jim Travers

✷ Smithsonian

ISBN 978-0-06-089144-2 (pb)

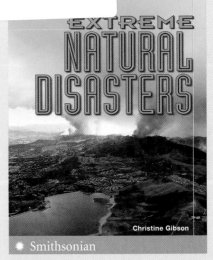

EXTREME NATURAL DISASTERS

Christine Gibson

✷ Smithsonian

ISBN 978-0-06-089143-5 (pb)

Available wherever books are sold.

 Collins

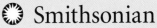 Smithsonian